SIMPLY DELICIOUS

Rose Elliot became a cookery writer by accident. She was planning to take a history degree when she met and married her husband and became involved in cooking, entertaining and having babies. It was while looking after the latter that she began scribbling down her recipes. These led to her first book, *Simply Delicious*, which in turn brought requests for cookery demonstrations. It was the invention of new ideas and recipes for these that provided the impetus for *Not Just a Load of Old Lentils*. All her recipes are tried out on her family, who lament that they only get a dish while it's being tested: once it's right (and they like it) it goes into a book – and she starts trying out something else!

As well as writing regularly in the leading vegetarian newspaper *The Vegetarian*, Rose Elliot broadcasts and appears on television. She is actively involved in the work of The White Eagle Lodge, a religious charity concerned with the spiritual values of life, meditation and spiritual healing. Its philosophy seeks to show how every individual can help to alleviate suffering and improve conditions around him.

D0680018

Simply
Delicious

ROSE ELLIOT

FONTANA/COLLINS

First published November 1967
by the White Eagle Publishing Trust
First issued in Fontana Books 1977
Third Impression September 1979

Copyright © by Rose Elliot 1967

Made and printed in Great Britain by
William Collins Sons & Co Ltd, Glasgow

CONTENTS

FOREWORD

Simply Delicious was the beginning of things for me. I'd left school at seventeen to cook at the retreat centre run by my family (vegetarian cooks are not easy to come by) and really enjoyed the challenge of making 'strange' vegetarian food look and taste appetising. That was back in 1962 and vegetarianism still had a very cranky and odd image. Although at the time I had been working to go to university, I was really very glad to shake the dust of school off my feet and took to the cooking with an enthusiasm and imagination that surprised everybody, soon finding I spent almost as much time writing out my recipes for interested guests as I did actually cooking.

A year later I married and the birth of my two daughters stopped me cooking professionally but gave me the opportunity to do what so many people had been urging me to do – write a recipe book. So I began testing, writing and sorting recipes, scribbling them on odd bits of paper between feeds, afternoon walks and bathtimes. The final collation and organisation of the menus was done on our sitting-room floor, piles of papers everywhere, throughout one night when my husband was away. The result was *Simply Delicious*, and I'll never forget the excitement of the publication and the surprise and thrill of the favourable reviews which followed.

The publication of *Simply Delicious* really opened up a new career for me, bringing cookery demonstrations, television, broadcasting and journalism, together with other books. I've become more and more interested in the whole subject of cookery, particularly the health,

economy and presentation aspects. To me cookery is
something of an art form; it's a joyous, creative activity,
a way of making people happy and healthy as well as
fulfilling in me the need for self-expression. I get great
satisfaction from blending different ingredients to produce just the right flavour; from putting together colours,
textures and flavours. It gives me tremendous pleasure
just to work with bright colours – vivid red beetroot,
orange carrot, rich, shiny green peppers, pale, yellow
avocado: these immediately stir the imagination. And
then there is the excitement of texture; of putting crisp
with creamy, crunchy with smooth and finding the whole
dish come alive.

People often ask me how I get my ideas. Initially it is
the challenge of creating something really delicious
without meat or fish which gets me going. I love to see
people's surprised faces when confronted with a vegetarian meal which is really good to eat and worthy of a
quality wine. Then I find I get a lot of ideas just looking
round a market or food shop and thinking about new
ways of using the things I see there. I enjoy developing
an idea and will often try out a recipe many times until
it is just right, but I don't really like cooking the same
things over and over again once they are right: by then
I'm busy with the next idea! There always seems to be
something new to try, some new taste to explore.

Just as *Simply Delicious* started me off on my career, so
I like to think of it as a good book from which to start
learning about vegetarian cookery. It gives all the basic
information on becoming a vegetarian and it tells you
the things you want to know when you start cooking –
things like how long vegetables take to cook, for instance.
It's written from practical experience and the recipes are
mostly the tried and tested family ones on which I got
my own grounding in vegetarian cookery; or they're
favourites which friends and the people I've cooked for
have passed on to me in exchange for mine. Amongst

them are some which are entirely original, such as the vegetarian sausage rolls, mushroom and tomato savoury, the mushroom nut flan and the asparagus and almond ring. The cashew nut and celery timbale which I also thought up is another favourite. At first I used to make it in a mould and bake it, then one day I didn't have time and found it was really much nicer (and quicker) served as it was, but I'm afraid the name 'timbale' stuck, even thought it really isn't, in the form I've given it!

The publication of *Simply Delicious* didn't stop me experimenting and trying out new ideas. Soon I found myself writing another cookery book, *Not Just a Load of Old Lentils*. Most of the recipes in *Not Just a Load of Old Lentils* are my own inventions and many of them are ones I find especially suitable for entertaining. That book has more detail on the nutritional aspects of the vegetarian diet and answers to all the questions people ask about it. Then there is a section of TVP (textured vegetable protein) which wasn't on the market when I wrote *Simply Delicious*. And whereas *Simply Delicious* is arranged in the form of menus because people told me that they found it difficult at first to think in terms of putting together a complete vegetarian meal, *Not Just a Load of Old Lentils* is arranged under the more orthodox headings, soups, salads, etc. The idea is that once you've got the hang of vegetarian meal planning from *Simply Delicious* you'll be able to put together your own menus from some of the more exotic dishes in *Not Just a Load of Old Lentils*! People tell me they have favourite recipes in both books and one lady said she keeps them both by her bed to read in the night because they help her to go to sleep – a use I hadn't thought of, I'm bound to say! Anyway, I hope you'll like both books and find them really practical and helpful.

January 1977   ROSE ELLIOT

P.S. My two daughters are now 10½ and 12, have never eaten meat or fish and are very healthy and energetic on their completely vegetarian diet.

I

FOODS, FLAVOURINGS, EQUIPMENT AND MEAL PLAN

Whatever the reason for becoming a vegetarian, if this way of life is to be happy and permanent it must be practical and able to stand up to the pressures of modern life. Therefore the food should be health-giving; it should look and taste delicious; and above all it should be simple and quick to prepare. The recipes and way of life described in this book are the ones which have evolved in our family over thirty years or more and have been found to fulfil these requirements.

Basically a vegetarian diet is one avoiding all foods which have involved the slaughter of animals, but includes cheese, dairy produce and eggs.

Many of the ordinary foods on the market are suitable for vegetarians. All those free from the products of slaughtered animals are listed in the 'Vegetarian and Vegan Food Guide' obtainable from either of the addresses listed on page 155.

In the ordinary meat diet only about half the protein intake is derived from animal flesh; the rest is supplied by milk, eggs, cheese, bread and cereals. A vegetarian diet, therefore, means a simple and normal diet with vegetable protein foods replacing the flesh part of the meals. These vegetable protein foods are mainly nuts and pulses (dried beans, lentils, etc.), all of which can be made into attractive savouries. Thus a meat diet may be simply translated into a vegetarian diet as shown below. The foods marked * may be bought from Health Food Stores, and the address of your nearest Health Food

Store may be had from The Vegetarian Society (UK) Ltd., at Parkdale, Dunham Road, Altrincham, Cheshire, or 53 Marloes Road, Kensington, London, w.8.

Main Protein Foods

Meat, fish, poultry, luncheon meats, fish and meat pastes are replaced in the vegetarian diet by:

1. NUTS*

Almonds, brazils, barcelonas, hazels, pinekernels and walnuts all provide an excellent source of protein comparable to meat protein. They can be made into savouries and desserts as described in the later chapters of this book, or can be eaten as they are in salads, or with cereal for breakfast. Cashew nuts and peanuts are also usually considered under this heading, although these really belong to the pulse group. Cashews are not rich in protein, and the addition of eggs, dried milk, cheese or other protein rich ingredient is recommended.

All these nuts may be bought by the pound, already shelled, from Health Food Stores and many grocers and supermarkets. They can also be bought by mail order at a substantial saving on quantities of 5 lbs. from some firms. (See advertisements in vegetarian magazines.)

They may also be used in the form of nut creams*, with desserts, in salad dressings, and in invalid and baby cookery.

There is a variety of canned nutfoods*; of these we prefer Granose 'Nuttolene'* and 'Sausalatas'* and in our experience both are unfailingly popular with children. Ready made rissole mixes* are useful for quick savouries.

Various nut butters* and pastes* are available for use in sandwiches; our favourite spread is 'Tartex'*.

2. PULSES

Pulses generally are not so rich in protein as are nuts

and are best reinforced from protein-rich sources such as milk, eggs, etc. Items coming under this heading are:

Lentils. We use the little red Egyptian lentils obtainable from any grocer. Used with other proteins, either in the savoury or in another course of the meal, they are nutritious and a good source of iron.

Soya beans, unlike other pulses, are rich in protein, but have a distinctive flavour not always acceptable to the Western palate. They are however delicious served in a richly flavoured sauce. They need to be soaked for 24 hours followed by long, slow cooking. It is possible to buy canned soya beans in tomato sauce* and these make a quick protein-rich savoury course.

*Soya flour** can be used to add protein to all kinds of dishes. It is best to buy this in small quantities as it tends to go sour once opened.

Butter beans, haricot beans, sweet corn, peas, dried and fresh are all useful sources of protein but not of a very good quality, so these foods need to be used in conjunction with other protein foods as previously suggested.

3. YEAST

Yeast is rich (about half its weight) in protein, but it is only palatable in small quantities. In its dried, powdered or flaked form it can be sprinkled over breakfast cereal (see Chapter II), or added to savouries lacking in protein, such as lentils. We use plenty of yeast in bread, at least 2 oz. to 2 or 3 lbs. flour, as this greatly increases the food value of the bread. Yeast extract is used for flavouring all types of savouries and gravies. Different brands are available from grocers and Health Food Stores, and replace meat extracts and stock cubes.

4. DAIRY PRODUCE

Dairy produce is a fine source of protein, as in the meat diet, but is perhaps used with more imagination. Under this heading come:

Cheeses of all types, including cottage and cream cheeses. We find cheddar best for cooking, but some of the more unusual types bring variety to salads.

Eggs are best when they are from hens on free-range*. Although these are a little more expensive than the battery ones, this is compensated for by the relative cheapness of the nuts and pulses in comparison with meat. They are not always easy to obtain but a list of farmers supplying these may be had from the Vegetarian Societies.

Milk supplies protein and vitamins in the vegetarian diet, as in the normal meat diet.

Dried milk powder is obtainable in various brands from Health Food Stores, and most grocers stock Cadbury's 'Marvel'. Added to puddings, drinks, savouries, and sprinkled over breakfast cereals it is a good extra source of protein. (See the section on balance of the diet, page 42).

Yoghourt is another source of protein It can be sweetened to taste with honey and served as a sweet or at breakfast either with, or in place of, cereal. Many of the commercial yoghourts are rennet based and therefore vegetarians prefer to use the natural yoghourt* or, more cheaply, as we always do, make it from yoghourt culture.

Cereals

In a balanced vegetarian diet, white flour, macaroni, polished rice and white breakfast cereals are replaced by the following natural cereals which retain the flavour and goodness usually removed by processing and refining:

1. 100% STONEGROUND WHOLEMEAL FLOUR*

Throughout this book, the flour used is 100% stoneground plain wholemeal. We use this flour for all purposes, and it is possible to make beautifully light cakes, biscuits and puddings with it (see Chapter VII). It is to some extent an acquired taste, but once accustomed to it, most people find its flavour far superior to white flour.

Various types of self-raising wholemeal flour are obtainable from Health Food Stores and some grocers and bakers, but it is simpler to buy plain and add the necessary baking powder.

A selection of wholemeal bread, biscuits and cakes is available at many Health Food Stores.

2. WHOLEMEAL MACARONI AND SPAGHETTI*

These can replace the white variety in all recipes. They take a little longer to cook but the flavour is delicious.

3. BROWN RICE*

We use natural brown rice instead of polished white rice in all recipes. It has a good flavour, but needs careful washing and takes a little longer to cook than the white rice. It should be used in combination with other protein foods.

4. WHEAT*

This can be bought in the form of grains (make sure they have not been treated with pesticide sprays). The grains can be milled to the required fineness in an electric coffee mill and eaten with, or in place of, cereal for breakfast, or they can be sprouted (see page 39) and served as a delicious and unusual addition to salads.

5. WHEAT GERM*

This is the protein containing heart of the wheat which has been extracted during the milling of white flour. While it is not a balanced food like the cracked wheat, it is useful for adding extra protein to dishes, and also as a breakfast food. Obtainable from Health Food Stores under its own name, or from chemists under the names 'Froment' and 'Bemax'.

6. WHOLEWHEAT FLAKES*

These are a pleasant breakfast food, similar to corn-flakes but made from the whole of the wheat, therefore more flavoursome and nutritious.

Cooking Fats and Oils

Lard, suet, dripping and whale-oil-based margarines are replaced in the vegetarian diet by:

1. PURE VEGETABLE COOKING FAT

Various brands are available, including Nutter*. Shortex is obtainable from Co-operative Stores. As with margarine and cooking oils, those suitable for vegetarians are listed in the Vegetarian and Vegan Food Guide (see page 155).

2. SUET*

Nut suets are available from Health Food Stores and make an excellent substitute for animal suet.

3. PURE VEGETABLE COOKING AND SALAD OILS

These are readily available and include Mazola and Twirl as well as many other brands listed in the Vegetarian and Vegan Food Guide' (see page 155).

4. MARGARINE

It is important to use a pure vegetable one such as Kraft Superfine, Tomor, Alfonal, Goldana, Co-op Soft Margarine, or Flora; for further information consult the Vegetarian and Vegan Food Guide (see page 155).

5. BUTTER

Used in the vegetarian diet in the same way as in the ordinary meat diet.

Sugars and Sweetenings

Over-refined white sugars are largely replaced in the vegetarian diet by the following, although we use white sugars in some dishes where the delicate flavour or colour would otherwise be spoiled:

1. HONEY

This is a nutritious, natural form of sweetening which can replace refined white sugars in many recipes.

2. BARBADOS SUGAR*

This real brown sugar is quite delightful, with a rich flavour; it can be used on cereals and in many recipes instead of white sugar; it is good in cakes, puddings and breads. It may be bought from Health Food Stores, or Whitworth's pure cane sugar can be obtained from many grocers and supermarkets.

Raw sugar chocolates and confectionery are obtainable from Health Food Stores.

Jelling Agents

Gelatine is replaced in the vegetarian diet by agar agar, gelozone and carrageen moss. These products are made from seaweed and are as effective and easy to use as gelatine; they have added advantages in that they set much more quickly and also contribute useful minerals to the diet.

1. AGAR AGAR

We find agar agar the most useful. It is a fine tasteless powder, and very easy to use. One level teaspoonful of agar agar will set half a pint of liquid; it is sprinkled gradually over the boiling liquid and stirred until dissolved.

2. GELOZONE

Gelozone is similar to agar agar, but it will not make a clear jelly and has rather a strong flavour. One level teaspoonful will set half a pint of liquid. It should first be dissolved in a little cold water and the hot liquid poured over it.

3. CARRAGEEN MOSS

Carrageen moss is the actual seaweed; it is useful for making junkets and blancmanges but does not set stiffly enough for cold soufflés and moulds which need to be turned out. It has a pleasant, delicate natural flavour. A good handful of carrageen moss (half a cup) will set one pint of liquid. It is washed and boiled with the liquid for 5 mins., and the liquid is then strained off, flavoured, and left to set.

Fruit and Vegetables

1. FRESH FRUIT AND VEGETABLES

Most people these days know of the value of fruit and vegetables, and vegetarians are no exception. They make full and varied use of vegetables, and have at least one salad meal of raw vegetables a day. They cook vegetables to retain as much flavour and goodness as possible (see Chapter IV). Those who find it difficult to digest raw salads can take instead the juice of fresh vegetables, either in canned unsweetened form, or by use of an electric juicing machine.

Where possible, compost-grown unsprayed vegetables* are used.

2. DRIED FRUITS

These are used extensively in the vegetarian diet, often replacing the canned fruits; they can be soaked overnight and eaten with, or instead of, cereal for breakfast (see page 16); or chopped and added to salads (see page 37); or can form the basis of many delicious desserts (see Chapter IV). Apricots, bananas, peaches, pears, prunes, figs and dates can all be obtained from Health Food Stores, or often from grocers and supermarkets.

3. CIDER VINEGAR

This usually replaces the ordinary malt vinegars in the

vegetarian diet, and is said to have health-giving properties. In any case, it has a pleasant flavour, and can be obtained from many ordinary grocers and super-markets.

Herbs and Spices

The natural flavours of the nuts and vegetables used in the vegetarian diet blend well with all types of herb and give great scope for the imaginative cook. The following notes give some guidance as to the most common uses of the herbs in the vegetarian diet. The list is long, and we have listed the herbs as far as possible in order of usefulness. Even if you only have one or two of the herbs this makes a good start from which to build a collection, perhaps buying a new herb periodically and experimenting with it in as many dishes as possible, noting the effect. These herbs and spices may be obtained from good grocers or Health Food Stores.

MIXED HERBS

Adds flavour to nearly all savouries, especially nut roasts. Also useful in stews and gravies.

PARSLEY

Useful in its dried form in practically all savouries, especially cheese ones. Fresh, it is attractive for garnishing, added to salads and soups at the last minute. A valuable source of vitamins and iron.

BAY

A leaf in stews, casseroles, soups and white sauces enriches the flavour.

MINT

Delightful fresh in salads, and with new potatoes and peas.

CHIVES

Use fresh, chopped in salads, with cream cheese, as a garnish for savouries, especially cheese ones, and soups.

GARLIC

Wipe a cut clove of garlic round the salad bowl; add to cheese and to tomato dishes, but use discriminatively as it can easily overpower the delicate flavour of the nuts and vegetables.

BOUQUET GARNI

Consisting of a bay leaf, a few sprigs of parsley and thyme, can be bought ready made up into little muslin bags. Gives a delicious flavour to stews, soups and casseroles.

BASIL

The 'tomato' herb. A pinch in all tomato dishes brings out the tomato flavour.

THYME

Good in stuffings and nut savouries. A pinch in gravies adds to the flavour. Fresh thyme is good chopped in salads.

SAGE

Good in nutmeat stuffings. A little fresh sage chopped in salads is unusual and delicious. It is good with cream cheese.

MARJORAM

A powerful herb; just a pinch in nut dishes, mushroom dishes and stuffings gives a distinctive flavour. Good with lentils.

ROSEMARY

Use this with the canned nutmeats; a pinch in a stew gives a delicate flavour, and used fresh and sparingly in salads, especially with grated carrots, it is piquant and unusual.

TARRAGON

Use fresh and chopped in salads, also in hollandaise sauce, and any dish with asparagus.

CHERVIL

Use lavishly in soups, especially clear vegetable soups. Also good in omelettes.

SUMMER SAVOURY

Excellent with any bean dish.

From the above it will be seen that as well as the dried herbs it is also useful to have a supply of fresh herbs for use in salads, and for garnishing. These are best planted as near the kitchen door as possible for easy use. If you have no garden, why not grow some of them in pots and keep them on the kitchen window-sill? We would suggest parsley, mint and chives for a start, and any of the following which appeal: marjoram, rosemary (nipped back to dwarf it), sage, thyme, chervil and tarragon. These are simple to care for and as pretty as pot plants – but much more useful.

SPICES used in the diet are similar to those used in the meat diet, and we find the following particularly useful:

SALT

The biochemic salt* or pure natural sea salt* is preferable to the ordinary table salt.

PEPPER

Freshly ground black pepper has much more flavour than the white variety, and has health-giving properties which are lacking in the latter. Pepper grinders are easily obtainable and are simple and quick to use.

CELERY SEED
Imparts a delicate flavour of celery to nutmeats, rissoles, soups, sauces, casseroles and gravies.

CORIANDER SEED
Gives a piquant flavour to soups, especially onion, celery and pea soup. Also good in curries, apple and celery dishes. Tie seeds in a little piece of cloth and remove before serving.

DILL
Very good with cashew nuts; also with tomatoes, cucumber and potatoes.

NUTMEG
Best freshly grated, but the ready-ground variety is simpler to use. Nutmeg improves the flavour of creamed or mashed potatoes, creamed root vegetables, spinach, sprouts, egg custards; use also in nut savouries.

CLOVES
Stuck in a piece of onion they impart flavour to soups, bread sauce and white sauces. They are also delicious in apple dishes.

PAPRIKA
Especially useful as a quick, attractive and colourful garnish to such things as mashed potato, white soups, cheese dishes and any savoury which is rather pale in colour.

MUSTARD
A pinch in cheese dishes improves them.

CAYENNE PEPPER
This is good with cheese dishes as a change from mustard, and is also nice with cream cheese, but it needs to be used sparingly as it is rather hot.

CURRY POWDER

Apart from its obvious use, a pinch adds flavour to gravies.

CARAWAY SEED

Good in tomato soups and sauces, and sprinkled over loaves or potatoes before baking.

TURMERIC

Adds a fine golden colour and delicious flavour to curries.

CINNAMON

Use in sweet dishes, and especially with apples or rhubarb.

GROUND MACE

A little in white sauces is good, also in white nutmeats.

MIXED SPICE

For fruit cakes and puddings. Also use a pinch with stewed fruit, or sprinkled over custards.

Useful Equipment

Most homes already have the equipment necessary for changing to the vegetarian diet. Essentials are:

NUT MILL

This can be a hand one, or for the keen vegetarian a little electric model which will mill nuts and quickly grate carrots and other vegetables for salads is a great time-saver. Choose a mill which has a fairly fine grater (such as the type you would grate cheese on if you wanted it fine) and this will be excellent for nuts. It will be a help to find a place for it where it can remain ready for use, so that you do not constantly have to be getting it out of a drawer and fixing it on the table before you can start the preparation of a meal. This is what takes the time!

MOULI or SIEVE

Very useful for making soups and pulping lentils. The 'Mouli-Légumes' can be bought fairly cheaply at most hardware shops and is a sensible, practical piece of equipment.

BIRCHER-BENNER GRATER*

This is the best grater we have found for grating small quantities of cheese, carrots, almost anything.

TRELLIS GRATER

For making breadcrumbs. Obtainable from any hardware store.

Optional extras in this list are:

LIQUIDISER

Useful in the vegetarian kitchen, as in any other, but not essential.

COFFEE MILL

A small, simple coffee mill, electric or hand, is useful for grinding whole grains for the vegetarian breakfast, and for milling the less greasy nuts such as cashews, almonds and hazel nuts really finely, especially for invalids and babies.

ELECTRIC JUICE EXTRACTOR

Useful but not essential. Very helpful for people who cannot manage to eat the raw vegetables and salads in their natural form.

Meal Plan

The ideal meal plan is the one which suits each individual best, and allows the principles of diet outlined to be put into practice. The following routine which we have evolved may serve as a guide, and a basis for variations according to particular needs.

On rising: Cup of tea, or half a glass of fresh orange juice, or hot water and lemon juice.

Breakfast: This may of course be varied according to taste. It can consist of a selection of wholewheat cereals, dried fruits, fresh fruit, nuts, yoghourt, with milk and honey or brown sugar for sweetening, followed, if a cooked breakfast is desired, by a light egg dish, or perhaps grilled mushrooms. The meal can be completed with wholemeal bread or toast, butter and marmalade or honey, with milky tea, coffee, or dandelion coffee, or fruit juice.

The salad meal, lunch or dinner, as convenient: Soup followed by a large mixed salad of all types of fruit and vegetables in season, with nuts or cheese as protein, or a simple cooked cheese, nut or egg savoury, hot or cold. Baked jacket potatoes may be served if desired, the meal finished with a simple sweet or piece of wholemeal fruit cake.

The cooked meal, lunch or dinner, as convenient: Fresh grapefruit, melon or fruit juice, followed by a cooked nut, pulse, cheese or egg savoury, and conservatively cooked vegetables (but not potatoes if these have already been served with the salad meal) followed by a simple sweet or fresh fruit.

Before retiring: A milky drink, tea, coffee, dandelion coffee or other beverage.

The plan in this book is to take each of these meals in turn, breakfast, lunch and dinner, and explain in detail the usual form this meal takes in the vegetarian diet, and then give menu suggestions and recipes in detail for everyday and special occasions.

All quantities given are for four people unless otherwise stated.

II

BREAKFAST

The vegetarian breakfast is usually an uncooked one consisting of a wholemeal cereal dish followed by wholemeal bread or toast with butter and honey or marmalade, and completed with fresh fruit if desired. If a cooked meal is preferred, a light mushroom, tomato or egg dish (see pp. 20–32, also p. 147) can follow the cereal.

THE CEREAL DISH

Wholemeal cereal such as Weetabix, Sunnybisk, Frugrains or Shredded Wheat, can form the basis of the cereal course, and any of the following foods can be added, varying the combinations day by day. Those who are not used to these foods can, perhaps, start by adding them to their normal breakfast cereal, trying them out one by one, and experimenting with the new flavours.

SOAKED FRUIT

This is prepared the night before, by washing a selection of dried fruits – apricots, prunes, pears, apple rings, peaches, sultanas or raisins, and just covering them with boiling water. Add a little thinly pared lemon or orange rind if liked, and leave until morning. The fruit can be eaten as it is, or can be lightly cooked for about five mins. (Be careful not to overcook.) Enough can be prepared for several days and the bowl kept in a cool place.

DRIED FRUIT

Raisins, sultanas, dates, figs and dried bananas can be added to the cereal foods and are a natural form of sweetening.

BARBADOS SUGAR

This unrefined sugar is a delicious and health-giving form of sweetening, which can be used on the cereal and fruit when required, replacing the usual white sugar.

CRACKED WHEAT OR WHEAT GERM

Cracked wheat is the wholewheat grains ground to the required fineness in an electric coffee mill[1] or special grinder. It is delicious, rich in vitamins, protein and minerals.

If this is not possible, wheat germ can be added to the cereal instead. Wheat germ has been extracted from the grains during the milling of white flour, and is rich in protein, but is not such a balanced food as the cracked wheat which has qualities which none of the separate parts contain.

DRIED YEAST

Dried powdered yeast, or flaked yeast, taken regularly lightly sprinkled over the cereal makes up for many deficiencies in a diet. About a tablespoonful daily is enough for average use, but when there is great depletion and nervous exhaustion, double that quantity is beneficial. If you find the taste unpalatable, yeast can be taken in tablet form with the breakfast, 6 to 12 tablets daily according to the brand selected.

YOGHOURT

This can be taken in place of cereal if preferred, either on its own or with dried or soaked fruit, honey, sugar or wheat germ.

DRIED SKIMMED MILK POWDER

An excellent source of protein which is delicious sprinkled over the cereal, or can be beaten into a morning glass of milk.

[1] See I on Useful Equipment.

HONEY

This can be used to sweeten the cereal instead of sugar. It is particularly good with yoghourt.

NUTS

The kernels of walnuts, almonds, brazil nuts or hazel nuts can be served with the cereal, either whole or chopped or grated in a mill.

WHOLEMEAL BREAD OR TOAST

A dish composed of a selection of these foods, with or without breakfast cereal as a basis, is a meal in itself, but can be followed by wholemeal bread (quickly and easily made as described on page 135), with butter and honey or marmalade.

FRESH FRUIT

Fresh fruit in season can complete the meal if desired.

TEA OR COFFEE

Most people like to have a drink with their breakfast. Ideally, tea and coffee have no place in a food reform vegetarian diet, but it is hard to find a really satisfactory substitute. Dandelion coffee is available from Health Food Stores, and is pleasant once one gets used to it. The instant type is as quick to make as instant coffee; alternatively, juice can be taken.

If these foods are prepared the night before and set out on an hors d'oeuvre dish with several compartments, or several individual dishes or jars, the family can help themselves in the morning. The dishes then can be topped up ready for the next morning, thus saving much time, washing up and effort, and ensuring that the family start the day with a health-giving and sustaining meal.

III

THE SALAD MEAL, SOUPS AND PACKED MEALS

Most vegetarians like to have at least one meal a day consisting of raw vegetables and fruits made into a salad, often preceded by a soup, especially in winter.

In this busy age there seems little enough time for making the main part of the meal let alone a soup! This is especially so for vegetarians who do not have the advantage of instant stock cubes readily available to add flavour. Nevertheless, soup can play an important part in the diet, for if properly made it contains many minerals which might otherwise be lost. With a little planning (and especially with the aid of a liquidiser), soup-making need not be time-consuming and when soup is served the following courses can be relatively lighter. For days when there is no time for soup-making, many of the canned and packet soups on the market are vegetarian[1], and there are also some delicious block soups available from Health Food Stores.

We always save the water in which vegetables have been cooked. This makes an excellent stock, but vegetable water from greens should be used the same day as it turns sour if kept; and it should be remembered that potato water will make a soup cloudy. The outside leaves and stalks and trimmings of most vegetables can be cooked for an hour or so and the water strained off to provide stock. Do not be put off from making a soup

[1] Those suitable for vegetarians are listed in the Vegetarian and Vegan Food Guide obtainable from the Vegetarian Society (UK) Ltd at the address given on p. 155.

because there is no stock available, however, because ordinary water can be used and additional flavourings added later.

Ideas for salads appear alphabetically at the end of this chapter (see page 35). The soup and savoury menus given in the following pages can be eaten with any salad or combination of vegetables, prepared as directed. Or, of course, the salad can be served with grated nuts, cheese, or hardboiled egg or a cold cooked savoury.

Soups and Savouries for the Salad Meal

Menu 1

Potato and Watercress Soup

1 large peeled onion	1½ pints water or stock
1 lb. potatoes	salt and pepper
1 oz. margarine	¼ pint top milk or single
½ tsp. dill or marjoram	cream
(optional)	1 bunch watercress

Chop onion; peel potatoes and chop into small pieces. Lightly fry onion and potato in the margarine, with the herbs, for 5 mins. Add the water or stock and simmer for 30 mins. Liquidise or pass through a mouli. Season to taste and add top milk or cream and re-heat but do not allow to boil. Wash watercress, chop finely, and serve sprinkled over the soup. If cream or top milk is not available, or too rich, cook vegetables in ¾ pint of stock and add a pint of milk.

Cheese on Pineapple

4 oz. cream cheese	1 tbs. chopped onion or
4 oz. finely grated cheddar	chives
cheese	2 tbs. finely grated apple
pinch paprika pepper	4 large pineapple rings or
	8 small ones (canned)

Beat the cream cheese until soft, mix in the grated cheese, paprika pepper, chives and apple. Pile heaps of this mixture on the pineapple rings and serve immediately with a salad including lettuce, watercress or cabbage as available, and raw grated carrot or beetroot.

Menu 2

Carrot Soup

2 large carrots	1½ pints water
1 onion	pinch nutmeg
1 oz. margarine	salt and pepper
½ tsp. thyme	chopped parsley
1 tbs. plain flour	

Scrape and chop carrots; peel and chop onion; cook in margarine with thyme for 5 mins. but do not allow to brown. Stir in flour, add water. Cook for 30 mins., then liquidise or pass through a sieve or mouli. Season with nutmeg, salt and pepper. Add chopped parsley to garnish.

Cooked carrots and onion can be saved from a previous meal, and used to replace the raw carrots in the above recipe if an instant soup is required.

Savoury Macaroni Mould

4 oz. wholemeal macaroni	2 tbs. chopped fresh
1 small onion	parsley or 2 tsp. dried
1 level tsp. mixed herbs	parsley
2 oz. margarine	8 oz. hazel nuts, milled
1 egg	salt and pepper

Cook macaroni in boiling water until tender (about 20 mins.) and drain. Peel and chop onion and cook with herbs in the margarine until tender but not brown. Mix in all the other ingredients, turn into a buttered basin or mould, and steam for 1 hour. Serve cold in slices, accompanied by a green salad.

Menu 3

Tomato Soup

1 onion	1 tbs. plain flour
2 sticks celery	1 medium-sized can tomatoes
½ tsp. basil or mixed herbs	1½ pints water or stock
1 oz. margarine	sugar, salt and pepper to taste

Peel and chop the onion; wash and chop celery and fry gently with the herbs in the margarine for about 5 mins. but do not let them get brown. Stir in the flour, add the tomatoes and stock and simmer for about 30 mins. until the vegetables are tender. Pass through a liquidiser or sieve, return to the pan, add sugar, salt and pepper to taste.

Cheese Dreams

8 slices of wholemeal bread margarine	8 oz. grated cheddar cheese

Spread each piece of bread on both sides with margarine, and then sandwich them with cheddar cheese. Fry them gently until crisp and golden, and then turn them over and fry the other side. Serve hot, accompanied by a salad including tomatoes and lettuce or watercress as available. (No extra fat is needed in the pan for frying.)

Menu 4

Instant Soup

If you make it a habit always to cook a few extra vegetables, and to save them together with their water, they can be made into soup for the following day in about as little time as it takes to open a can of soup. Put them into a liquidiser (or through a mouli), heat them up with any combination of the following: a little Marmite, a pinch of garlic salt, a little chopped parsley or mint, a pinch of paprika pepper, a knob of butter, perhaps a little mushroom ketchup or a squeeze of lemon juice, a little milk or cream; season well with salt and pepper, and you have a delightful soup which can be thickened with a little cornflour, or brown flour if desired.

Stuffed Peppers (Unfired)

2 green peppers	2 tbs. sultanas
8 oz. cream cheese	

Remove and discard core and all seeds from peppers, wash and dry them. Chop sultanas roughly, using a sharp knife. Beat cream cheese until smooth and stir in the chopped sultanas. Fill the peppers with this mixture, and then using a sharp knife slice the stuffed peppers into rounds about $\frac{1}{2}''$ thick, and serve garnished with a sprinkling of paprika pepper, and accompanied by a mixed salad including a green vegetable (as available), grated raw carrot or beetroot, and garnished with chopped fruits in season.

Menu 5

Leek and Potato Soup

2 leeks	$\frac{1}{4}$ pint top milk or single
1 medium-sized potato	cream
1 oz. margarine	1–2 tbs. chopped parsley
1 bay leaf	salt and pepper
$1\frac{1}{2}$ pints water	

Wash and chop the leeks, discarding the tough green leaves, but using as much of the green part as possible; peel and chop potato. Cook these very gently in margarine together with the bay leaf, for about 10 mins., stirring occasionally, but on no account let them brown. Add the water and cook gently for about half an hour, then sieve or liquidise. Return to the pan, add the top milk or cream, parsley and seasoning, but do not let it boil.

Unfired Nutmeat

4 oz. walnuts or hazel
  nuts
4 oz. cream cheese
½ tsp. paprika pepper

2 tbs. chopped chives
salt and pepper

Finely mill the nuts. Blend all ingredients together, adding a little milk or cream if mixture is too stiff. Form into a roll and leave in a cool place or fridge for half an hour. Serve in slices with tomato salad or celery and apple salad, and green salad in season.

Menu 6

White Onion Soup

4 onions
1 oz. margarine
2 pints water

4 tbs. Marvel
1 tbs. plain flour
salt and pepper

Peel the onions, chop very finely and cook gently in the margarine for 5 mins., then add the water, saving a little for mixing with the flour. Cook the onions for about 15 mins., when they should be tender but not soggy, then add the flour mixed with the water and stir in the Marvel. Season with salt and pepper and cook until slightly thickened.

Hazelnut Mould

1 medium onion
1 oz. butter or margarine
1 dsp. agar agar
¾ pt. vegetable stock or water
4 oz. hazelnuts

1 dsp. Barmene (or
  if using vegetable
  stock, 1 tsp.)
saltsp. garlic salt
pinch pepper

Finely grate onion and fry in fat until golden brown. Dissolve agar agar in a dessertspoon of cold water and gradually add to the vegetable stock (or seasoned water). Pour into onion and bring to boil for 5 minutes. Remove from the heat and add the hazelnuts which have been first placed in a moderately hot oven for about 10 minutes to loosen skins, then rubbed in a clean cloth to remove most of skins and milled finely. Add seasoning to mixture and cook for another 5 minutes. Pour into previously rinsed mould or moulds. If liked, moulds may be lined with slices of tomato and cucumber, in which case first brush mould with the mixture, then arrange the vegetables, then pour a little mixture over sides of mould and allow to set before adding the rest of the mixture.

Menu 7

Clear Vegetable Broth

1 stick celery	2 pints stock or water
1 large carrot	1 dessertsp. chervil
1 onion or leek	2 tbs. chopped parsley
½ oz. margarine	salt and pepper
1 bay leaf	1 tsp. Marmite

Chop the prepared vegetables finely and cut the onion into rings. Toss the vegetables in the melted margarine, add the bay leaf and chervil and stock and simmer for about 15 mins. until the vegetables are tender but whole. Add the chopped parsley, seasoning and Marmite. Serve at once.

Scotch Eggs

2 hardboiled eggs	2 oz. butter
leftover or canned nutmeat	1 tsp. mixed herbs
plus enough mixed grated	1 dessertsp. Marmite
nuts to make 1 lb. altogether	2 eggs
1 large onion	salt and pepper

Mix together nutmeat, herbs, Marmite and one of the

eggs. Roll mixture round eggs, egg and breadcrumb them, and fry in deep boiling fat until golden brown. Serve cut in half, garnished with parsley, and accompanied by a salad including any of the following in season: beetroot, carrots, cauliflower, celery, chicory, tomatoes.

Menu 8

Celery Soup

1 oz. margarine or butter
1 small onion
6 outside sticks from 1 head of celery
½ level tsp. celery seed
½ level tsp. coriander seed (optional)
1 level tbs. cornflour
1½ pints water or stock
¼ pint top milk or single cream

Melt the butter or margarine over a gentle heat, peel and chop the onion; wash and dice celery including any leaves and toss gently in the butter or margarine. Cook for 5 mins., then stir in the flour. Add water, and celery seed and coriander seed tied in a piece of muslin. Cook for 45 mins. Liquidise, (having removed muslin bag!) add seasoning to taste and the top milk or cream. Do not allow to boil. Serve immediately garnished with a fresh sprig of parsley.

Cheese Egg Flan

6 oz. wholemeal short-crust pastry
1 onion
4 oz. grated cheese
1 tbs. chopped parsley
1 egg
¼ pint milk
1 tomato (optional)
salt and pepper

Make pastry from 6 oz. plain wholemeal flour, 3 oz. vegetable fat, 1 teaspoonful baking powder and 1 table-spoonful cold water and line a flan dish. Peel and chop onion and cook in a little water until tender. Drain and put in flan case with cheese and parsley. Beat egg with milk, add seasoning, and pour over. Remove skin from tomato, cut into slices and place attractively on the top of the cheese mixture. Bake in hot oven, 450° F., gas mark 8, for 10 mins., then reduce heat to 300° F., gas mark 2, and cook for a further 30 mins. Serve hot or cold.

Menu 9

Mushroom Soup

2 onions	1 tbs. cornflour
8 oz. mushrooms	1½ pints water or stock
½ tsp. marjoram	½ pint milk
1 oz. margarine	salt and pepper

Peel and chop onions, wash and chop mushrooms, and cook with the marjoram in the margarine for 10 mins. Stir in the cornflour, add the water, and cook for 20 mins. Liquidise or pass through a mouli. Add the milk, season to taste with salt and pepper and reheat.

Brazil Nut Savoury Cake

1 medium onion	8 oz. brazil nuts, milled
1 tsp. mixed herbs	4 oz. soft brown breadcrumbs
2 oz. margarine	2 eggs
1 tbs. plain flour	salt and pepper
¼ pint milk	1 tbs. chopped parsley

Peel and chop the onion and fry with the herbs in the margarine for 10 mins. without browning. Stir in the flour and the milk, allow to thicken and then add all the other ingredients, seasoning to taste. Press into a greased 8″ sandwich tin and bake in a moderate oven, 350° F., gas mark 4, for 45 mins., until golden brown and crisp. Serve cold, with a mixed salad including tomatoes, onions (if liked), celery and green vegetables in season

Menu 10

Lettuce and Onion Soup

2 large onions	2 tbs. ground rice
2 large lettuces or the equivalent in outside lettuce leaves	1 pint water
	1 pint milk or milk and water
1 oz. margarine	salt and pepper
3 sprigs parsley	

Peel the onions; chop onions and lettuce into small pieces and cook gently in the margarine for 10 mins. without browning. Add parsley, ground rice and water, and cook for 30 mins. Liquidise or pass through a mouli. Add the milk or milk and water, salt and pepper and reheat.

Cheese and Pimento Savoury

1 medium onion	4 oz. grated cheese (preferably Cheshire)
2 oz. butter	
saltsp. celery salt or celery seed	½ small bottle tomato chutney or ketchup
pinch pepper	small tin tomatoes
pinch paprika pepper	small tin pimentos (red peppers)

Chop the onion *very* finely. Slightly warm butter and beat seasonings in, then mix in onion and grated cheese, chutney and tomatoes (mashed with a fork). Either cut the pimentos small or crush them with a fork and add to the above. Use either as a spread for sandwiches or scones or as a savoury on a green salad. If a small quantity is required, make half and use the rest of the pimentos in a rice, onion, sweetcorn and greenpea savoury.

Menu 11

Lentil Soup

1 oz. margarine	1 bay leaf
1 onion	½ pint milk
1 carrot	2 tsp. lemon juice
4 oz. lentils	1 level tsp. Marmite
1½ pints water	salt and pepper

Melt margarine in a large pan. Peel and chop onion, scrape and chop carrot and fry together until lightly browned. Add lentils, water and one bay leaf (if liked) and cook for 1 hour, or about 10 mins, in a pressure cooker. Pass through sieve or liquidise, return to pan, add milk, lemon juice, Marmite, and seasoning to taste.

Savouries on Toast

4 slices wholemeal bread	or 2 large cans soya beans
2 large cans Tartex	in tomato sauce
8 oz. mushrooms, fried	or 6 oz. grated cheese, ½ tsp. made mustard

Toast and butter the bread. Top with any of the following:

1. Thickly spread Tartex and fried mushrooms. Serve a protein-rich salad, soup or sweet with this
2. Heated soya beans in tomato sauce
3. Combine the grated cheese and mustard, press on top of the toast and heat under the grill until melted, bubbly and brown.

Serve with mixed salad, including apple, pear, celery, green pepper and grated carrots when in season.

Menu 12

Spinach Soup

1 lb. spinach	1 tbs. plain flour
1 onion	$\frac{1}{4}$ pint top milk or single
1 oz. margarine	cream
$1\frac{1}{2}$ pints stock	nutmeg
	salt and pepper

Wash the spinach thoroughly. Peel and chop onion and cook in the margarine for 5 mins. but do not brown. Add the spinach and stock, and cook for 30 mins. Liquidise or pass through a mouli. Add flour blended to a cream with the milk. Return to pan and bring to the boil, stirring. Cook for 2 mins. Add nutmeg, salt and pepper to taste.

Sausage Rolls

Sausages

4 oz. milled nuts (hazels, almonds, walnuts or a mixture)	1 tsp. Marmite
	1 tsp. basil
	1 egg, beaten
2 oz. cooked mashed potato	salt and pepper
2 medium onions, peeled, finely chopped and fried	

Special cheese pastry

4 oz. margarine and vegetable fat, mixed	1 tsp. baking powder
	3 oz. grated cheese
5 oz. plain flour	a little sweet chutney

To make the sausages, mix all the ingredients to a fairly stiff consistency. Place small rolls of the mixture on a greased baking sheet and bake in a slow oven at 325° F., gas mark 3, for 20 mins. Meanwhile make the pastry by rubbing the fat into the flour and baking powder and adding the cheese. Roll out carefully (it will be rather tacky), brush with sweet chutney. Put sausages on the pastry and wrap it round each to form rolls. Bake in a hot oven, 450° F., gas mark 8, for 10 mins., and serve hot or cold, with mixed salad including grated raw carrot, beetroot, turnip or swede and green vegetables available.

Menu 13

Cold Cucumber Soup

1 large cucumber	1 level dessertsp. arrowroot
1 small onion or shallot	4 tbs. cream or evaporated
1½ pints vegetable stock	milk
or water	salt and pepper
½ tsp. dill (optional)	1 sprig mint

Peel cucumber thinly and cut into small pieces; peel and chop onion and place both in a pan with the stock and dill. Bring to the boil and cover, simmer for 10–15 mins. Pass through a sieve or liquidiser, and return to the pan. Blend the arrowroot with a little milk or cream and stir into the mixture in the pan. Bring to the boil, stirring all the time, and cook for a few seconds until thickened slightly. Add seasoning to taste. Chill thoroughly, and serve in chilled bowls, garnished with a slice of cucumber and chopped parsley or fresh sprigs mint.

Cheese Soufflé

2 oz. margarine or butter	4 oz. cheddar cheese
1 heaped tbs. plain flour	salt and pepper
¼ pint milk	4 or 5 eggs, separated
¼ tsp. dry mustard	

Melt the butter in a pan; stir in the flour but do not brown; add the milk, stirring, and the mustard. Cook for 2 mins. Remove from heat, season, and mix in the cheese and egg yolks. Leave until cool, then fold in the stiffly

31

beaten egg whites. Turn into a greased soufflé dish and bake for 30 mins. in a moderately hot oven, 400° F., gas mark 6. Serve with tossed green salad, tomatoes or mushroom and potato salad when a substantial meal is required.

Menu 14

Pea Soup

1 large can garden peas	1½ pints water or stock
1 large onion	sugar, salt and pepper to
3 cloves	taste
6 sprigs fresh mint (or dried)	a dash of cider vinegar

Tip peas into pan. Add the onion with cloves stuck into it, the mint and water or vegetable stock. Cook until the onion is tender. Pass through a sieve or mouli, or put into a liquidiser. Flavour with salt and pepper. Add a dash of cider vinegar.

Bread and Egg Fritters

3 eggs
4 slices of wholemeal bread
½" thick, or as required
salt and pepper to taste

This dish is particularly popular with children and served with grilled tomatoes, makes a useful and nourishing breakfast for them.

Beat the eggs and pour them over the slices of bread, which have had the crusts removed. Let the liquid soak well in, then fry the bread in hot vegetable oil. Sprinkle with salt and pepper, and spread thinly with a little Marmite if liked. Serve immediately.

SALAD

So many varieties are available that it is possible with a little ingenuity to serve many different combinations throughout the year. Try to avoid thinking of salad purely in terms of a little bit of lettuce, half a tomato and a piece of beetroot. Use at least two different varieties of grated raw vegetable, such as carrot, swede, beetroot, cabbage (red and white), sprouts, cauliflower, broccoli, and other greens with one or two of the usual salad ingredients such as lettuce, chicory, endive, cress and tomato, varying them each day and garnishing with fresh fruit in season. Most salads are improved by being crisped in the salad container of the refrigerator.

The salad can be dressed with any of the following; in each case we find it helpful to make up enough for a whole week, and keep in a cool place to use as required.

Mayonnaise

1 egg yolk (at same temp. as oil)	salt
	¼ pint olive oil
½ level tsp. dry mustard	1 dessertsp. cider vinegar
½ level tsp. sugar	or lemon juice
good sprinkling freshly ground black pepper	

Mix the egg yolk with the mustard, sugar, pepper and a pinch of salt. Measure the oil into a jug and add drop by drop, beating all the time with a whisk. When the mayonnaise starts to thicken, the oil may be added a little more quickly. When really thick, add a little cider vinegar or lemon juice to thin it again to the right consistency. Keep in a screwtop jar in a cool place.

French Dressing

6 tbs. olive oil
2 tbs. cider vinegar or lemon juice
salt and pepper

Combine all together in a screwtop jar and shake vigorously until blended. Any of the following may be added for variety:

a pinch dry mustard
sugar or honey to taste
½ tsp. paprika pepper
1 small onion, chopped
1 tsp. chopped parsley or chives

Yoghourt Dressing

4 tbs. natural yoghourt
2 tsp. lemon juice
salt and pepper

Combine yoghourt and lemon juice and season to taste.

Honey and Cider Vinegar Dressing

1 tsp. honey
½ cup cider vinegar
salt and pepper

Mix all ingredients, stirring well.

Fruit Juice

Fresh unadorned orange or lemon juice, or lemon juice and honey makes an excellent quick dressing.

SOME SALAD SUGGESTIONS

BEANS

Tender French or runner beans can be cut into $\frac{1}{2}''$ lengths and added to the salad. Very tender broad beans (uncooked) are also delicious.

BEETROOT

Raw (1) Grate finely and toss in fresh orange or lemon juice, adding some sultanas and chopped mint if liked.

(2) Grate finely and mix with yoghourt for a delicious sweet-sour salad. Add sultanas if desired.

Cooked Slice thinly and mix with a little cider vinegar and barbados sugar.

CABBAGE

Choose small green, hearty cabbages, not the white, tough, flavourless 'salad' cabbages. Wash thoroughly in salted water, and then slice finely, or grate fairly coarsely. Dress with salt, fresh lemon juice and pepper.

CARROTS

Scrub to remove dirt, or scrape lightly if they are old. Serve young tender carrots cut into rings or matchsticks, or made into curls by paring off very thin layers lengthwise and leaving in cold water to curl up. Sprinkle with lemon or orange juice to prevent discoloration. Grate old carrots finely and squeeze orange juice over them; add a few sultanas, or some chopped fresh mint or rosemary for a delightful flavour.

CAULIFLOWER

Wash thoroughly, break into little florets, and serve raw.

DRESSED CAULIFLOWER

Blend 1 tablespoonful lemon juice and 2 tablespoonfuls olive oil, chopped chives or mint or parsley, and salt

35

in a bowl. Stir in finely chopped cauliflower and sprinkle with paprika.

CELERIAC

Choose small tender roots. Wash and scrape lightly. Grate finely and sprinkle with lemon juice.

CELERY

Wash all parts thoroughly. Use the leaves chopped in salads or in soups; the outer stems for cooking in soups or savouries or as a vegetable. Chop the tender stalks or cut them into 2″ lengths and slit down nearly to the base at $\frac{1}{8}$″ intervals and leave in cold water.

CELERY AND APPLE

Chop and mix together equal parts of celery and apple (with skin on if tender). Cover with freshly squeezed orange juice, and add coarsely chopped walnuts.

CHICORY

Wash thoroughly and cut into rings, or separate the leaves and serve whole, or slice the chicory lengthwise in halves or quarters.

CHICORY BOATS

Separate the leaves and fill each with a little finely grated carrot or beetroot, blended with a little fresh orange juice. Garnish with parsley.

COLE SLAW

Prepare cabbage as previously described, and mix with a little grated onion, lemon juice and cream or olive oil.

CORN ON THE COB

The very tender young kernels can be washed and served raw. Cooked fresh or canned sweet corn may also be served with salad.

CRESS

Wash watercress or American landcress thoroughly,

removing any tough stems or leaves. Use the stalks in soups. Cut the stalks of cress as low down as possible, and wash thoroughly.

CUCUMBER

Wash and peel thinly if the skin is tough, or flute the skin by drawing the prongs of a fork down the length; slice into rounds, cut into cubes, or grate coarsely.

DRESSED CUCUMBER

Prepare as above, slicing thinly. Sprinkle with salt, black pepper and $\frac{1}{2}$ teaspoonful dill. Stir in 2 tablespoonfuls plain yoghourt and 1 teaspoonful freshly chopped parsley.

ENDIVE

Prepare as for lettuce.

FRUITS

These are delightful in any salad. Apples, pears, pineapple, melon, banana, strawberries, raspberries, oranges, blackberries, peaches and grapes, may all be used. Wash well and remove skin or chop if necessary.

DRIED FRUITS

Prunes, dried apricots, raisins, dates, figs and sultanas are all good in salads. Soak the prunes and apricots overnight if desired, then drain and chop as necessary.

GREEN SALAD

Put 2 tablespoonfuls cider vinegar and 6 tablespoonfuls olive oil, a pinch of salt, and a grating of black pepper into a wooden salad bowl. Beat with a wooden spoon until the ingredients have combined. Then toss in pieces of lettuce, endive and any of the following when in season: chopped green cabbage, chopped sprouts, chopped kale or broccoli tops, chopped celery leaves, watercress, cress, corn salad, American landcress, spring onions, cucumber, green pepper, apple, french beans, tender young broad beans, walnuts, cubes of cheese, avocado slices, cubes of Nuttolene or other nutmeat of a firm texture, sliced egg, spinach leaves, nasturtium leaves, sorrel leaves, sprigs of cauliflower.

HERBS

Fresh herbs are delightful in a salad in small quantities and we always try to include at least one variety. Parsley, mint, chives, tarragon, rosemary, chervil, summer savoury, basil can be used as available. Wash thoroughly and snip into the salad with kitchen scissors.

LETTUCE

Choose crisp heads and wash in cold water. Break apart the leaves, using as many of the green outside leaves as possible (these are the richest in vitamins); save any very tough leaves to make into soup, or to cook like greens; very little need be thrown away. Shake the leaves dry in a salad basket or loosely gathered up in a clean tea cloth. Break the leaves into pieces. They can be served as they are or form the basis of a green salad.

LETTUCE WITH MINT

A good way of using the rather tough leaves. Chop these finely and mix with 1 tablespoonful finely chopped mint, 1 teaspoonful sugar and 1 tablespoonful cider vinegar. Season with salt and pepper.

MUSHROOMS

Choose small button mushrooms, wash in cold water, and trim the ends off the stalks. Slice thinly and use raw.

ONIONS

The green part of onions when they have sprouted may be washed and chopped and added to salads like chives for a subtle onion flavour. Peel ordinary onions and cut into thin rings. Cover with cider vinegar and leave to soak for several hours before using.

SPRING ONIONS

Wash well, skin off roots and green tops (use these in soups). Use whole or slice into rings.

PEAS

Shell and wash the peas. Serve sprinkled on the salad.

PEPPERS

Red or green peppers may be used. Slice in half, remove seeds, wash well, and chop flesh finely. Use raw.

POTATO SALAD

1 lb. cooked potatoes	4 tbs. mayonnaise
1 tbs. finely chopped or grated onion	little cream or top milk
salt and pepper	chopped parsley

Dice the potatoes – new ones are delicious. Do not overcook them or they may break up when mixed. Add the onion and season with salt and pepper. Thin the mayonnaise with a little cream or top milk and add to the potato mixture. With a fork toss the mixture until the potatoes are well coated with the mayonnaise. Serve garnished with chopped parsley.

RADISHES

Wash and trim off tops and tails. Add to the salad whole or sliced, or made into lilies by using a small sharp knife to slit the radish down from the tail end six times to form petals, and leaving in cold water to open out.

SPINACH LEAVES AND SPRING GREENS

Wash thoroughly and chop finely. Dress with French dressing (see page 34), or a dressing made from cider vinegar and a little honey (see page 34).

SPROUTED CORN

Grains of corn can be left in a little water for a few

days until they start to sprout little green shoots. They can then be washed and added to the salad; they have a pleasant fresh, nutty flavour.

TOMATOES

Wash, and peel if skin is very tough, then cut into quarters, or slices, or make into water-lilies by making zigzag cuts round the middle of each tomato using a sharp pointed knife. Pull the slices apart.

TOMATO SALAD

Peel one tomato per person, cut into quarters or eighths and put into a bowl in which has been mixed 1 teaspoonful brown sugar, pinch salt, ½ teaspoonful dried or 1 tablespoonful chopped fresh basil, 1 teaspoonful fresh parsley and 1 tablespoonful cider vinegar.

TURNIPS

Choose young tender ones. Peel thinly and grate finely. Dress with a little squeezed lemon juice and season with salt and pepper.

PICNICS AND PACKED MEALS

A health-giving picnic or packed meal should be carefully planned to ensure a proper balance of protein, carbohydrates and vegetables. When packing these meals we have found small polythene containers to be ideal, one for salad, and one for sandwiches and cake and other oddments which can be placed straight into the container without wrapping in foil or greaseproof paper. If it is more convenient, a packed lunch can be assembled in the evening and left in the fridge or cool place overnight, thus saving time in the morning.

Many of the savouries suggested in this chapter may be served cold as the protein part of the meal or wholemeal sandwiches made with a generous amount of any of the following protein rich fillings:

Cream or cottage cheese with
    Chopped nuts and raisins
    Chopped pineapple (canned or fresh)
    Sultanas
    Sliced cucumber and chopped parsley
    Chopped chives
    Chopped lettuce

Grated cheese with
    Sweet chutney
    Grated apple
    Chopped raw onion
    Tomato and parsley mixed to a paste

Scrambled egg with
    Cress
    Chives

Peanut butter with
    Chopped raw onion
    Raw grated carrot
    Sliced banana

Finely grated hazel nuts (or walnuts or almonds)
    creamed with butter and a little yeast extract
Equal quantities of nuts and raisins minced together
Cheese and pimento savoury (see p. 28)

Serve the savoury with a generous amount of salad, which will keep beautifully fresh in a polythene container. Any vegetables in season may be used, and could include cabbage, kale, broccoli, lettuce, endive, young spinach leaves, celery leaves, cress, watercress, chicory, cucumber, radish, scraped raw carrot, cauliflower, tomatoes.

The meal can be concluded with a piece of wholemeal cake, a handful of nuts and raisins, an apple, pear, orange, banana or a few grapes, and perhaps a piece of raw sugar chocolate.

IV

THE COOKED MEAL – VEGETABLES

Introduction

Most people like cooked vegetables and a hot savoury for the main meal of the day, either eaten in the middle of the day or in the evening, whichever is more convenient. We like to start this meal with fresh fruit juice, grapefruit or melon, followed by a savoury made from nuts, pulses, eggs or cheese, together with conservatively cooked vegetables, and completed with dessert or just fresh fruit. In the following section recipes are given for the savoury course with its appropriate sauce and sweet. Each savoury has been planned with its sweet course to form a balanced meal, but varied menus can, of course, be created by using different combinations. When creating new menus the following points may be helpful:

Balance of the Meal

It is generally agreed that a balanced meal should consist of protein, carbohydrate and vitamin-containing vegetables or fruit.

I. PROTEIN

In the vegetarian diet this is derived as already described from nuts, eggs and cheese. The pulses and cashew nuts (which are usually classed with nuts but really belong to the pea family) also provide protein but as already said in Chapter I, with the exception of soya beans, are not such a rich source and need to be used in combination with whole cereals or with milk, dried milk, soya flour, eggs or cheese, to provide the necessary amount of protein. This extra protein can be incorporated into the savoury dish, or it can be included in the following sweet dish.

2. CARBOHYDRATE

This is usually provided in the cooked meal by the inclusion of potatoes or rice. Unless cooking for a very hungry family, it is unnecessary to serve potatoes with rice or macaroni dishes, and if the family is trying to reduce excess weight it is advisable to omit potatoes when serving a dish with breadcrumbs or pulses in it, or else to serve the potatoes and omit the breadcrumbs from the recipe. (See Chapter X on Slimming.)

Some of the puddings in this section are substantial ones, suitable for family meals, and can always be replaced by fresh fruit or a lighter sweet by those who do not need such a filling meal. Sweets which are protein rich and therefore suitable for following a low protein savoury, are marked with an asterisk

3. VEGETABLES AND FRUIT

These can either be a delicious source of essential vitamins and minerals, or they can be practically inedible and devoid of nourishment – depending on the cooking. At the end of this chapter we have given full instructions for cooking different types of vegetables to conserve their flavour and food value (see page 78).

Green vegetables – all varieties of cabbage, kale broccoli, sprouts, spinach, turnip tops when available – are especially valuable in the diet *and should be served as often as possible*. At times of the year when it is difficult to obtain plentiful fresh vegetables, one can make up for this deficiency by serving fresh fruit desserts, and also by insisting on the fruit juice start to the meal. Oranges as described in the recipe section make a delicious sweet and they are cheap and easily available during the winter.

The juices with which we start the cooked meal are easily made with the aid of an electric juicing machine, or frozen orange juice can be used, or canned (preferably unsweetened) juices are excellent and provide a refreshing start to the meal, as well as being a source of vitamin C.

Vegetarian Food for One

The fact that only one member of a family is a vegetarian need not prove too difficult. We have found a small steamer ideal in such circumstances, for the whole meal can be cooked in this, with perhaps a savoury steaming in the top with potatoes and other vegetables which need long cooking, while the greens or peas or other quickly cooked vegetables can be added to the water in the bottom half of the steamer and cooked for a short time at the end.

Time-Saving Methods

All the savouries in this section are quick to prepare, and they are the ones which we have found most practical. The recipes can be taken in any sequence, but we have arranged them so as to provide variety. When planning meals it saves a great deal of time to think in terms of two or three days at a time. For instance, cook enough potatoes to have boiled or creamed one day, and then fried or in a savoury, or as a topping for shepherd's pie the next day.

The following are ways of thinking and planning ahead which we have found helpful:

1. Mill extra nuts for use in savouries or sprinkled over puddings.
2. Cook an extra hardboiled egg and use as a quick garnish the next day.
3. Cook extra lentils, soya beans or rice and keep in fridge ready for a savoury another day.

4. Cook extra vegetables ready for a soup the next day.
5. Cook extra potato, either to fry the next day or to incorporate into a savoury.
6. Rub in at least 1½ lbs. flour and 12 oz. fat at a time (adding three heaped teaspoonfuls baking powder if using plain flour) and keep this in the refrigerator. It stays fresh for at least a fortnight and is then ready for pastry with the addition of water; or with the addition of sugar for a quick crumble topping; or, with the addition of grated cheese, as a savoury crumble topping to vegetables in cheese sauce; or as the basis of a fruit cake (see recipe in Chapter VII).
7. Grate extra cheese, for use in any savoury, sprinkled over the top of vegetables, or in sauces.
8. Always make a good quantity of brown sauce (gravy). Get this to the *roux* stage, that is, with fat and flour mixed together, and add the Marmite or other seasoning and just a little *cold water* (*not* vegetable water for this sours quickly). This thick mixture will keep easily for a week in the refrigerator. Then it can be used a little at a time, diluted with fresh vegetable water.
9. Make enough white sauce for two days, perhaps using it in a savoury one day and with vegetables the next day.
10. Make extra nutmeat so that it can be served hot one day, and cold, or in a pie, stew, batter or rissoles another day.

It sounds obvious, but a great deal of time can be saved by carefully planning the kitchen so that everything is near to hand, with a spice and herb shelf by the cooker, and all the cooking implements near, with knives for vegetable preparation close to the sink, and bowls and baking tins and flour in a group where you normally prepare bread, cakes and pastry. It helps to keep much-used utensils (kitchen scales, for instance) always out, and if there is enough space this saves a surprising amount of time.

The menus in this chapter have been planned in sets of seven, or one week's recipes, although they can of course be used as required.

The following list includes all the items needed for the recipes in this section, ensuring that you will have all the ingredients to hand for any particular recipe.

Canned Foods

Apricots
Baking powder
Bicarbonate of soda
Butter beans
Cocoa
Drinking chocolate
Evaporated milk
Golden syrup
Gooseberries
Meatless steaks*
Nuttolene*
Pineapple pieces
Sausalatas*
Soya beans in tomato
 sauce*
Tomatoes
Tomato juice

Fruit and Vegetables

Apples, cooking and des-
 sert
Bananas
Carrots
Cauliflower
Celery
Green beans

Leeks
Lemons
Marrow
Mushrooms
Onions
Oranges
Parsley
Peas, frozen
Potatoes
Rhubarb
Tomatoes

Dairy Produce

Butter
Cheese, Cheddar
Cream
Eggs
Milk

Jars and Bottles

Almond essence
Cider vinegar*
Green vegetable colouring
Honey, clear
Jam, apricot or raspberry
Mango chutney
Marmite or Barmene

* Obtainable from Health Food Stores.

46

Nut cream, almond*
Redcurrant jelly
Sweet chutney
Tomato chutney
Vanilla essence
Vegetable oil

Packets

Agar agar*
Almonds*
Angelica
Apricots, dried
Arrowroot
Barbados sugar*
Brazil nuts*
Brown rice*
Butter beans, dried
Carrageen moss*
Cashew nuts*
Caster sugar
Chocolate, plain raw
  sugar*
Coconut, desiccated
Cornflour
Currants
Custard powder
Dates, cooking
Flour, plain 100% whole-
  meal stoneground
Glacé cherries
Granulated sugar
Ground almonds
Ground rice
Hazel nuts*
Jellies, lemon*
Lentils
Margarine

Porridge oats
Soya beans, dried*
Soya flour*
Sponge cakes (unless using
  home-made)
Sultanas
Toasted almonds
Toasted crumbs
Walnuts*
Wholewheat flakes*
Wholewheat macaroni*

Herbs and Spices (if used)

Basil
Bay leaves
Cayenne pepper
Celery seed
Cinnamon
Cloves
Coriander seed
Curry powder
Dill
Garlic
Mace, ground
Marjoram
Mint
Mixed herbs
Mixed spice
Mustard
Nutmeg, whole and
  ground
Paprika
Parsley
Pepper (black)
Rosemary
Sage
Salt
Turmeric

* Obtainable from Health Food Stores

Savouries and Sweets for the Cooked meal

Menu 1

Brown Nutmeat

2 large onions	1 heaped tbs. plain
2 cloves garlic	flour
2 oz. mushrooms (optional)	¼ pint water or stock
2 oz. margarine	2 eggs, beaten
½ tsp. rosemary ⎫	8 oz. milled walnuts or
½ tsp. basil ⎬(optional)	hazel nuts
½ tsp. celery ⎭	4 oz. soft wholemeal
seed	breadcrumbs
1 tsp. Marmite	salt and pepper

Chop finely the onions, garlic and mushrooms if used, and fry in the margarine with the herbs and celery seed until lightly browned. Stir in the Marmite and flour. Add the water and cook until thickened, then add the beaten eggs. Cook for 2 mins., then add the milled nuts and breadcrumbs, and season to taste. Well grease a 1-lb. loaf tin or casserole, and pile in the mixture. Cover with greased paper or foil and bake in a moderate oven, at 350° F., gas mark 4, for 1 hour. Or the nut roast can be rolled in breadcrumbs or crushed cornflakes, dotted with cooking fat, and baked at 375° F., gas mark 5, for 45 mins. Serve with brown gravy and redcurrant jelly. Serve brown nutmeat with carrots or cauliflower in white sauce, and a green vegetable.

Brown Gravy

1 oz. fat	Marmite
1 oz. plain flour	curry powder
½ pint water or	salt and pepper
vegetable stock	celery seed or mixed
	herbs

Melt the fat and stir in the flour. Cook over a moderate heat until the flour is deep brown. Add the water (preferably water strained from the vegetables) and Marmite to taste, and stir well. Season with curry powder, celery seed or herbs, and cook over a low heat until required. Simmering improves this gravy and it is worth making it early on, when preparing the meal, to give the flavours time to blend well.

Apple Whip

1½ lbs. cooking apples	2 tbs. honey
¼ pint water	1 tbs. lemon juice
3 cloves	angelica
1 small tsp. coriander seed (optional)	grated lemon peel to decorate
1 small can evaporated milk	

Peel, core and cut the apples into pieces and cook in the water with the cloves and coriander seed (tied in a piece of muslin) until the apples are pulpy – about 5 mins., then sieve or liquidise. Beat the evaporated milk until double in bulk and a stiff foam, fold in apple, honey and lemon juice. Divide between four glasses, and decorate each with a little grated lemon rind and pieces of angelica, or top with whipped cream if desired.

Menu 2

Sausalatas

1 large can Sausalatas
toasted crumbs
cooking oil or fat

Wash the jelly off the Sausalatas and discard this. Roll the Sausalatas in the toasted crumbs. Heat 2 oz. vegetable fat or oil in an oven tin on top of the stove and roll each Sausalata in the oil until well covered. Put

Sausalatas at top of a hot oven, 450° F., gas mark 8, and cook for 40 to 45 mins. They will then be brown and very crisp and quite delicious either hot, or cold in salad. Serve with creamed potatoes, brown gravy (see page 48), peas or canned soya beans in tomato sauce or other protein vegetable, or follow by a protein rich pudding.

Fruit Crumble

1½ lbs. cooking apples or	¼ pint water
½ lb. dried apricots	2 tsp. grated lemon
2 oz. sugar	rind

Soak the apricots overnight; peel, core and cut the apples into thin slices. Put layers of apples, or apricots, and sugar into an ovenproof dish, with the water and sprinkle with lemon rind.

Crumble

12 oz. 'rubbed-in'	4 oz. margarine
mixture or 8 oz.	4 oz. sugar
100% plain	pinch cinnamon
wholemeal flour	salt

Rub margarine into flour, (or use rubbed-in mixture) mix in sugar, salt and cinnamon. Top apple mixture with crumble, and bake in a moderate oven, 350° F., gas mark 4, for 20 mins.

Menu 3

Butter Bean and Tomato Pie with Cheesy Crust

1 can butter beans or	1 tbs. tomato chutney
½ lb. dried butter beans	1 14 oz. can tomatoes
1 large onion	1 tsp. lemon juice
½ tsp. basil	salt and pepper
2 oz. butter or margarine	6 oz. cheese shortcrust

If using dried butter beans soak overnight and then cook until tender. If using canned butter beans drain off water. Peel and chop onion and fry lightly with the herbs in the butter or margarine for 10 mins. Add the beans, chutney, tomatoes and lemon juice, season carefully, put into an ovenproof dish and cover with cheese shortcrust. Bake in a hot oven at 450° F., gas mark 8, for 15 mins. Serve with a green vegetable (not peas or beans).

Cheese shortcrust

Make this as ordinary shortcrust using 6 oz. plain flour; 1 heaped teaspoonful baking powder; 3 oz. fat; 4 oz. grated Cheddar cheese.

Apples and Nuts*

4 dessert apples	honey to taste
2 oranges	whipped dairy or
4 oz. walnuts	nut cream

Wash the apples but do not peel. Grate them into a bowl and cover with the juice from the oranges. Chop or mill the nuts, add to the mixture and sweeten with honey to taste, if necessary. Pile into four individual glasses and top with whipped dairy cream or nut cream.

Menu 4

Cheese Puffs

6 oz. finely grated cheddar cheese	$\frac{1}{2}$ tsp. paprika pepper
2 oz. chopped walnuts	2 eggs, separated
1 heaped tbs. chopped parsley	salt to taste

Mix the grated cheese with the walnuts, parsley and paprika pepper and egg yolks. Beat the egg whites to a stiff froth and fold into the mixture. Season with the salt, shape lightly into small balls and fry a few at a time in deep boiling fat until golden brown – 3 to 4 mins. Drain on crumpled kitchen paper and serve immediately, with tomato sauce. Cheese puffs go well with a root vegetable.

Tomato Sauce

1 small onion	1 tbs. plain flour
1 clove garlic	1 small can tomato juice
1 oz. margarine	salt, pepper and sugar
½ tsp. basil	

Chop onion and garlic finely and cook in the margarine with the basil until tender but not brown – about 10 mins. Stir in the flour, add the tomato juice and cook for 2 mins. Pass through a mouli or liquidiser if desired. Season to taste with salt, pepper and brown sugar.

Fruit Flan

6 oz. shortcrust pastry (see page 127)	⅛ pint syrup (from apricots)
large can apricots	1 heaped tsp. cornflour or arrowroot
glacé cherries (if liked)	juice of 1 orange

Line a flan tin with pastry, prick the bottom and bake at 450° F., gas mark 8, for 10 mins. Strain off and reserve the juice from the apricots and rinse the fruit well under cold water. Arrange apricots with the glacé cherries if liked, in the cooled flan case. Heat syrup in pan. Mix cornflour with the orange juice and pour the boiling syrup over the mixture. Return to pan and stir until thickened. Pour the sauce over the apricots and allow to cool.

Menu 5

Nutmeat and Mushroom Batter Pudding

4 oz. plain flour
1 level tsp. baking powder
3 eggs
½ pint milk
8 oz. nutmeat (canned or leftover)

1 medium onion
4 oz. mushrooms
1 tsp. mixed herbs
2 tbs. cooking oil or cooking fat

We use more eggs than in the usual recipes in order to increase the protein value of this dish.

Preheat the oven to 400° F., gas mark 6. Sift the flour and baking powder into a large bowl; make a depression in the flour and drop in the whole eggs, one by one, gradually beating into the flour until the mixture is really smooth; add the milk gradually. Heat the oil in a baking dish in the oven; add diced nutmeat, chopped onions and mushrooms, together with the herbs and cook in the oven until the vegetables are tender. While the fat in the dish is sizzling hot, pour on the well-beaten batter (the more it is beaten the better) and bake for 20 mins. Serve immediately.

Baked Bananas

4 bananas
sugar
whipped cream

Place the bananas, unskinned, on a dry baking sheet and bake at 375° F., gas mark 5, for about 20 mins., until the skins are completely black. Cut away ½″ strip of skin down the complete length of the banana, loosening the skin slightly. Sprinkle a little sugar over them and top with a generous amount of whipped cream.

Menu 6

Cashew Nut Fritters

2 medium-sized onions
2 oz. butter
½ tsp. dill (optional)
2 oz. wholemeal flour
¾ pint milk
1 egg

4 oz. finely milled cashew
 nuts
2 tsp. lemon juice
salt and black pepper
flour
toasted crumbs

Chop the onions finely. Melt the butter over a gentle heat in a large pan, add the onions and dill and cook gently until the onions are soft but not brown (about 10 mins.). Stir in the flour and milk. Mix well, and cook very gently for 2 mins. until thickened. Add ground cashew nuts, lemon juice, seasoning and cook for 3 mins.; when cold divide into eight portions, dip each into flour then beaten egg, and coat with toasted breadcrumbs. Flatten each piece so that it is about ⅓" thick. Fry pieces on both sides in hot fat until golden brown. Drain well on kitchen paper and serve garnished with lemon wedges and with parsley sauce, and follow by a light protein rich sweet. Suggested vegetables: chipped potatoes, braised tomatoes and green salad (or cooked greens).

Parsley Sauce

1 oz. margarine
1 oz. cornflour

½ pint milk
2 heaped tbs. chopped
 parsley

Melt the margarine, add the cornflour, cook for 2 mins., gradually stir in the milk, heat gently until thickened, stirring all the time. Beat in the parsley and season to taste.

Lemon Whip*

½ pint water
4 level tsp. agar agar
4 oz. caster sugar or
  honey to taste

finely grated rind and
  juice of 2 lemons
2 egg whites
chopped walnuts
whipped cream

Heat water to boiling and stir in agar agar, sprinkling it over the liquid a teaspoonful at a time. Add sugar or honey, heat until dissolved. Draw off heat. Leave until beginning to thicken, then whisk in lemon juice and rind. Beat till frothy. Beat egg whites till stiff and fold in. Pour into serving dishes. When set, garnish with walnuts, and cream if desired.

Menu 7

Macaroni or Spaghetti with Tomato Sauce

8 oz. wholemeal macaroni
  or spaghetti
1 large onion
1 clove garlic
2 oz. margarine or olive
  oil

1 tsp. basil
medium-sized can tomatoes
salt and pepper
1 tsp. sugar
1 tsp. cider vinegar
6 oz. grated cheese

Cook macaroni or spaghetti in boiling water until tender – about 15 mins. Peel and chop onion and garlic and fry in the margarine or oil with the basil for 10 mins. Add the tomatoes and cook for 5 mins. Mash or sieve the mixture, and season with the salt, pepper, sugar and cider vinegar. Drain the macaroni or spaghetti and toss it in a little butter. Pour the sauce over the macaroni and surround with grated cheese. Serve with green vegetables.

Stewed Apples

2 lbs. cooking apples
¼ pint water

2 cloves
4 tbs. clear honey

Peel, core and slice the apples. Cook gently in the water with the cloves until tender. Add honey to taste and serve hot or cold, topping with whipped cream and toasted almonds if liked.

Menu 8

Stuffed Marrow

1 medium-sized marrow	¼ pint water
2 large onions	1 egg
4 oz. mushrooms (optional)	4 oz. hazel nuts milled
2 oz. margarine	4 oz. breadcrumbs
1 tsp. sage	salt and pepper
1 tbs. plain flour	

Peel and chop the onion; wash and chop the mushrooms if used, and fry in the margarine for 10 mins. but do not brown. Mix in the other ingredients, cook for 2 mins. and then add salt and pepper to taste. Cut marrow in half lengthwise and remove skin and seeds. Stuff with the nut mixture and put halves together again, securing them by wrapping in greased paper. Heat a little fat or oil in a tin, place the marrow in this and cook in a moderate oven, 350° F., gas mark 4, for ¾ to 1 hour, until marrow is tender. (The length of time will depend on the relative toughness of the marrow.) Serve with apple sauce, roast potatoes and green beans, and follow with a protein-rich sweet.

Apple Sauce

2 medium-sized cooking apples	4 tbs. sugar butter
4 tbs. water	cinnamon

Peel, core and slice the apples, and cook in the water

until tender. Add sugar to taste, a small knob of butter and a pinch of cinnamon.

Queen's Pudding*

4 oz. soft bread or cakecrumbs	3 eggs
1 pint milk	2 tbs. apricot or raspberry jam
2 oz. sugar	2 oz. desiccated coconut
1 tsp. vanilla essence	

Place the breadcrumbs in a greased ovenproof dish. Warm the milk, in which the sugar has been dissolved, and flavour with the vanilla essence. Beat the eggs thoroughly and add to the milk; pour over the breadcrumbs and cook very slowly in a moderate oven, 325° F., gas mark 3. When set, spread the top with apricot or raspberry jam and sprinkle with the coconut. This pudding must on no account boil or overcook. It is a good idea to set the dish in a pan of water in the oven, as a precaution against this eventuality.

Menu 9

Cheese and Onion Roll

8 oz. shortcrust pastry (see page 127)	6 oz. cheddar cheese salt
3 large onions	tiny pinch cayenne pepper

Roll pastry into a large oval. Cook peeled and chopped onions in a little water until tender but not mushy – about 10 mins. Strain to remove excess liquid, which can be kept for the gravy. Grate cheese, mix with the onions, season to taste and pile on to the pastry. Fold over pastry to make a roll. Bake in a hot oven, at 450° F., gas mark 8, for 15 mins. Serve with brown gravy (see page 48), braised tomatoes and green beans or green leaf vegetables.

Apricot Fool

8 oz. dried apricots	¼ pint custard
½ pint water	¼ pint double cream
rind of ½ orange	

Soak the apricots in the water overnight with the thinly pared orange rind. Next day they should be fairly tender; if not, cook gently until tender, then liquidise or sieve. Mix with custard and whipped double cream. Sweeten to taste. Serve cold.

Menu 10

Tomato Nut Mince

1 large onion	salt and pepper to taste
½ tsp. basil	8 oz. finely milled walnuts
2 oz. margarine	or hazel nuts
2 14-oz. cans peeled	4 oz. soft wholemeal
tomatoes	breadcrumbs
	2 tbs. sweet chutney

Chop the onion finely and fry with the herbs in the margarine until brown. Add the tomatoes and all the other ingredients. Cook gently for 20 mins. Serve garnished with small triangles of fried bread and parsley. Suggested vegetables: mashed potatoes, leeks, carrots or beans.

Ground Rice Fluff

2 oz. ground rice	½ tsp. almond essence
1 pint milk	sugar or honey to taste
1 egg, separated	nutmeg
½ tsp. vanilla essence	redcurrant jelly or Ribena

Mix the ground rice to a smooth paste with a little of the milk. Scald the rest of the milk and pour over the ground rice, stirring all the time. Return to pan and cook gently for 5 mins., still stirring, and being careful not to burn the mixture. Remove the pan from the stove and carefully mix in the beaten egg yolk; return to stove and cook for 2 mins. Add essences. Sweeten with sugar or honey. Fold in the lightly beaten egg white. Serve hot or cold, sprinkled with nutmeg and topped with a little redcurrant jelly or Ribena.

Menu 11

Egg Rissoles

2 oz. butter or margarine
1 heaped tbs. cornflour
½ pint milk
salt and pepper
pinch mace or nutmeg
2 tbs. grated cheese

4 hardboiled eggs
2 tbs. well-chopped fresh parsley
a little plain flour for coating
cooking oil

Melt butter in a pan; blend in the cornflour. Remove from heat and add the milk slowly, stirring. Bring to the boil, stirring all the time till the mixture thickens. (It must be a stiff mixture.) Add the seasoning and grated cheese and allow the cheese to melt before adding the well-chopped eggs and parsley. When the mixture has cooled a little, shape into rissoles. Coat with flour and shallow-fry both sides in very hot fat until golden brown. Serve with grilled tomatoes and other vegetables in season.

Treacle Sponge

4 oz. plain flour
4 oz. vegetable shortening
4 oz. golden syrup

1 tsp. bicarbonate of soda
¼ pint milk

Cream the fat with the golden syrup and add the flour, mixing well. Dissolve bicarbonate of soda in the milk.

Mix quickly with the syrup mixture, pour into a well-greased basin, tie down with foil, and steam for 1½ hours. Serve with hot syrup poured over.

Menu 12

Hazel Nut Pie

1½ lbs. potatoes	¼ lb. hazel nuts, milled
2 large onions	¾ pint milk
1 clove garlic	salt and pepper
2 oz. butter	cornflakes or wholewheat
1 tsp. paprika	flakes
½ lemon	margarine
	grated cheese

Cook potatoes until tender, then mash well with a little butter and seasoning. Chop onions and garlic and cook gently in the butter until soft but not brown – 10 mins. Add mashed potatoes, paprika, the rind and juice of half a lemon, the milled hazel nuts and milk. Season with salt and pepper, put into a greased casserole dish, cover with cornflakes, dot with margarine and a sprinkling of grated cheese. Cook in a slow oven, 325° F., gas mark 3, for 20 mins. Hazel nut pie is best served with braised or canned tomatoes and another vegetable in season.

Apple Cake

12 oz. 'rubbed-in' mixture or	2 oz. currants
⎰ 8 oz. plain flour and	4 oz. brown sugar
⎱ 4 oz. margarine and 1 heaped	½ tsp. mixed spice
tsp. baking powder	1 egg
8 oz. chopped peeled cooking	a little milk
apples	

Rub fat into flour which has been sieved with the baking powder, or use 'rubbed-in' mixture. Add spice,

60

apples, currants and sugar, with beaten egg and enough milk to give a soft dropping consistency. Bake for 1 hour in a slow oven, 300° F., gas mark 2, and serve hot with brown sugar and custard, or cold, sliced and buttered.

Menu 13

Lentil and Onion Fritters with Mint Sauce

12 oz. lentils	salt and pepper to taste
1 large onion	1 tbs. lemon juice
1 oz. vegetable fat	1 egg

Put dry lentils into a pint pudding basin and cover with water. Put into a steamer and steam for $\frac{1}{2}$ hour. (For quick cooking lentils can be just covered with $\frac{1}{4}''$ water and simmered till all the water is absorbed—about 20 mins.). Stir from time to time. Chop the onion finely and cook in the fat for 10 mins. but do not allow to brown. Pass lentils through a mouli or sieve, then mix in the fried onion and all the ingredients, making a fairly stiff paste. Roll into shapes on a floured board and fry on both sides in hot shallow fat until crisp and golden brown, either on top of the stove or in a moderate oven. Serve with mint sauce, braised tomatoes and a green vegetable. Follow with a protein rich sweet.

Mint Sauce

2 heaped tbs. fresh chopped mint	1 tbs. brown sugar
1 tbs. boiling water	2 tbs. cider vinegar

Put mint into a small jug and cover with the boiling water. Add the sugar and cider vinegar. Stir before serving.

Quick Chocolate Mousse*

4 oz. plain raw sugar	3 eggs
chocolate	½ tsp. vanilla essence
½ oz. butter	

Break the chocolate into a basin and set over a pan of hot water. Stir until melted and smooth, then add butter, egg yolks and essence. Stir until blended and then remove from heat. Stiffly whisk the egg whites and fold them carefully into the chocolate mixture. Spoon into glasses and chill until set firm and ready to serve.

This is useful for serving after a low protein savoury.

Menu 14

Cheese Kedgeree

4 onions	½ pint milk
2 oz. margarine	pinch dry mustard
1 small cooking apple	pinch nutmeg
8 oz. brown rice	6 oz. grated cheese
1½ pints water	salt and pepper

Peel and chop the onions and cook in the margarine until soft but not brown – about 10 mins. Add the peeled and grated apple. Wash and pick over the rice, removing any hard pieces, and add to the onions, together with the water. Bring to the boil, put a lid on the pan and simmer very gently for 20 mins. or until rice is tender. Add the milk, mustard, nutmeg and grated cheese. Season to taste and serve immediately, garnished with tomato and parsley. Serve with a green vegetable or green salad.

Fruit Compote

½ lb. dried apricots	2 bananas, chopped,
pinch cinnamon	or other fresh fruit
2 tbs. sultanas	in season
small can pineapple pieces	2 level tsp. arrowroot

Soak the apricots in $\frac{1}{2}$ pint of water overnight with the cinnamon and sultanas. Next day simmer for 15 mins. Add the canned fruit, fresh fruit and the arrowroot blended with a little cold water. Cook for 5 mins. and serve hot or cold, with cream and chopped nuts. It may be sweetened with a little honey if desired.

Menu 15

White Nutmeat

This is a delicately flavoured nutmeat in contrast to the brown nutmeat in Menu 1, page 48.

1 onion	2 eggs
2 oz. margarine	8 oz. milled nuts (almonds,
1 tsp. mixed herbs	brazils or cashews)
1 tbs. plain flour	4 oz soft wholemeal bread-
$\frac{1}{4}$ pint milk or water	crumbs
	salt and pepper

Peel and chop the onion. Melt the margarine in a large saucepan and add the onion and herbs. Cook gently with the lid on the pan for 10 mins. but do not allow the onion to brown. Add the flour and stir well; add the milk and cook gently until thickened. Beat in the eggs, cook for 2 mins., then add the nuts, breadcrumbs and seasoning. Put the mixture into a well-greased 1-lb. loaf tin or casserole dish, cover with greased paper or foil, and bake in a moderate oven, 350° F., gas mark 4, for 1 hr. Or the nut roast can be rolled in breadcrumbs or crushed cornflakes, dotted with cooking fat, and baked at 375° F., gas mark 5, for 45 mins. Turn out on to a large plate and serve with gooseberry sauce.

Gooseberry Sauce

$\frac{1}{2}$ lb. gooseberries cooked till tender	1 oz. butter
	1 tbs. plain flour
or 1 small can gooseberries	sugar and salt to taste

Pass gooseberries through a sieve, or liquidise. Melt the butter in a pan, add the flour, stir well, then add the gooseberry purée and cook gently until slightly thickened. Season to taste with salt and sugar, and serve hot or cold.

Vanilla Ice-Cream with Chocolate Sauce

Bought or home-made ice-cream (as follows) may be used for this dish.

Vanilla Ice-Cream*

¼ pint milk
1½ oz. caster sugar
1 egg, beaten

¼ tsp. vanilla essence
¼ pint double cream

Make a custard by heating together the milk and sugar and pouring over the beaten egg. Return to the pan and cook over a low heat until thickened, stirring all the time. Stir in the vanilla essence and allow to cool. Whisk the cream lightly and strain in the custard. Place in frozen food compartment of fridge for half an hour, then remove and whisk thoroughly. Return to fridge and freeze until firm but not hard.

Chocolate Sauce

4 tbs. drinking chocolate
¼ pint water

½ oz. butter
1 tbs. top milk

Make sauce by heating together drinking chocolate and water and simmering for 10 mins. Add butter and top milk and serve hot or cold poured over the ice-cream.

Menu 16

Nutmeat and Vegetable Pie

2 carrots
2 onions
4 sticks celery
4 tomatoes canned or fresh
2 oz. margarine
1 tsp. mixed herbs
2 tbs. plain flour

1 level tsp. Marmite
juice from canned tomatoes plus water or stock to make ½ pint
1 tbs. sweet chutney
salt and pepper
large can Nuttolene or 12 oz. nutmeat
6 oz. shortcrust pastry (see page 127) or mashed potato

Prepare the vegetables, cut into small pieces and fry gently in the margarine with the herbs for 10 mins. Blend in flour and Marmite. Add water and cook for about half an hour until vegetables are tender. Add chutney, nutmeat cut into dice, and season to taste. Top with pastry or mashed potato and bake in a moderate oven, 375° F., gas mark 5, for 30 mins.

Muesli

juice of 2 oranges
4 eating apples
2 tbs. sultanas

2 rounded tbs. milled cashew nuts or almonds
2 rounded tbs. porridge oats
4 tbs. top milk or single cream

Put the orange juice into a large bowl and grate the apples into this. Add all ingredients with enough top milk or cream to moisten, and a little honey to sweeten if necessary. Alternatively, use the juice and grated rind of half a lemon, sweetened to taste with honey.

Menu 17

Green Pea Cutlets

1 onion	2 tsp. brown sugar
2 oz. margarine	2 tsp. cider vinegar
1 tsp. marjoram	3 oz. soya flour
1 lb. packet frozen peas	salt and pepper
1 tbs. fresh mint (chopped)	1 egg
or ½ tsp. dried mint	toasted crumbs

Peel and chop the onion and cook in the margarine with the marjoram until tender – 10 mins. Cook the peas in a little water until tender – 5 mins., then strain and pass them through a mouli. Mix them with the onions, add the mint, sugar, cider vinegar, soya flour and salt and pepper. Shape into rounds, dip in beaten egg (if serving with the suggested lemon meringue pie use the egg yolks for this) and coat with crumbs. Fry in shallow fat on top of the stove, or on the top shelf of a moderate oven 375° F., gas mark 5, until crisp on both sides. Serve with brown gravy, (see page 48) mashed potatoes and root vegetables, and follow with a protein-rich sweet.

Lemon Meringue Pie*

1 flan case	juice and grated rind of 2 lemons
½ pint water	sugar or honey to taste
2 level tbs. cornflour	2 egg whites ⎫
	4 oz. caster sugar ⎬ for the meringue

Make a flan case using 6 oz. wholemeal flour, 3 oz. vegetable fat, 1 teaspoonful baking powder, or 9 oz. 'rubbed-in mixture', 1 tablespoonful cold water, and bake blind. Put the water in a pan and bring to the boil. Mix the cornflour with the lemon juice and rind, pour the boiling water on to the mixture and return to the pan. Stir until thickened, sweeten to taste. Pour into the flan case. Meanwhile beat the egg whites until very stiff, fold in the sugar, pile on top of the lemon, being careful to bring the meringue right to the very edges (otherwise it will go soft and 'leathery' in cooking). Bake at 250° F., gas mark ½, for 1½ hours, until meringue is crisp. Serve cold.

Menu 18

Cheese Egg Pie

1 heaped tbs. cornflour	2 oz. grated cheese
1 pint milk	6 hardboiled eggs
1 bay leaf or pinch mace	1 lb. creamy mashed
knob of butter	potatoes

Mix the cornflour with a little of the milk to make a thin creamy consistency. Put the rest of the milk in a pan with the bay leaf or mace and bring to the boil, then remove bay leaf and pour the milk over the cornflour mixture, stirring all the time. Tip back into pan, add the knob of butter and cook gently till thickened, still stirring, then beat in the cheese and remove from the heat. Season to taste. Chop the eggs and stir into the sauce. Turn into a fireproof dish and top with the creamy mashed potatoes. Rough up the surface with a fork or pipe some decorative whirls of potato on top. Place in a moderate oven, 350°F., gas mark 4, and cook for 20 mins. Serve with braised tomatoes and other vegetables in season.

Jellied Apple with Sultanas

1 vegetarian lemon jelly	2 tbs. sultanas
¾ pint water	whipped cream or nut cream
2 dessert apples	angelica

Grate the apple coarsely and mix with the sultanas. Divide between four glasses, top with lemon jelly and allow to set. Serve topped with a whirl of whipped cream or nut cream and angelica leaves, and hand round sponge finger biscuits with it.

Menu 19

Meal-in-One-Pan

1 oz. margarine	½ vegetable marrow
4 medium-sized potatoes, peeled and chopped	(when in season) or 4 carrots, peeled and chopped
2 onions, peeled and chopped	1 bay leaf
1 medium size can tomatoes	salt and pepper
4 sticks celery, chopped (when in season)	1 large can Nuttolene a few green beans (when in season)

Melt margarine in a large pan and add all the vegetables (previously peeled and chopped in fairly small pieces) and cook them with the bay leaf very gently for about ten mins., stirring from time to time. Then add the can of tomatoes, salt and pepper to taste, and a little vegetable stock if necessary to make more gravy. Simmer until tender, add the Nuttolene, heat through and then serve; or serve without the Nuttolene and with the following nut dumplings. A little more liquid will be required if nut dumplings are used.

Nut Dumplings

6 oz. plain flour	2 oz. milled nuts
salt and black pepper	1 gill water
2 oz. margarine	

Season the flour with the salt and black pepper. Rub in the margarine. Add the nuts and well mix with the water. Shape into balls the size of walnuts, drop balls into the *boiling* liquid and cook for 10 minutes. Serve immediately or the dumplings will go hard. If the gravy is not boiling the dumplings will disintegrate. They can, of course be cooked separately in a little boiling stock if desired.

Almond Creams*

½ cup carrageen moss	½ tsp. almond essence
1 pint milk	1 egg white
green vegetable colouring	ground almonds
2 tbs. clear honey	whipped cream or nut cream

Wash the carrageen thoroughly and heat with the milk in a pan. Simmer *gently* for 5 mins., then strain, and add the green colouring, honey and almond essence to the strained milk. Beat egg white until stiff but not dry, and fold into the almond mixture. Pour into individual dishes and allow to set. Sprinkle thickly with ground almonds and top with whipped cream or nut cream.

Menu 20

Mushroom and Tomato Savoury

8 oz. soft breadcrumbs	8 oz. tomatoes
4 oz. milled nuts (any type)	salt and pepper
4 oz. margarine	1 tsp. marjoram
8 oz. mushrooms	(optional)

Fry the breadcrumbs and milled nuts in 3 oz. of the margarine, stirring frequently until golden and crisp. Wash and roughly chop the mushrooms; wash and quarter the tomatoes; fry together in the rest of the margarine for 5 mins. Grease an ovenproof dish and fill with alternate layers of the mushroom mixture and the crumb mixture, seasoning each layer with salt, pepper and marjoram (if used), and ending with the crumb mixture. Bake for 30 mins. in a moderate oven, 375° F., gas mark 5, and serve with a green vegetable. Follow with a protein rich sweet.

Trifle*

1 small can evaporated milk	4 small sponge cakes
¼ pint top milk	4 tbs. red jam
2 oz. sugar	¼ pint double cream
2 eggs, beaten	(optional)
½ tsp. vanilla essence	chopped almonds
½ tsp. almond essence	

Make a custard by heating the evaporated milk, top milk and sugar and pouring over the eggs, stirring. Return the mixture to the pan and cook over a gentle heat, stirring all the time (but do not allow to boil) until custard thickens. Add essences. Crumble the sponge cakes into a glass dish; melt the jam with a little water and mix it thoroughly with the sponge cakes. Strain the hot custard mixture over the sponge cakes and leave aside to cool. When ready to serve, cover the top with lightly whipped cream and scatter with chopped roasted or blanched almonds.

Menu 21

Vegetable Curry

½ lb. leeks	2 oz. vegetable fat
1 small cauliflower	1 dessertsp. curry powder
2 small onions	½ pint water
1 small cooking apple	pinch coriander seed
½ lb. peeled potatoes	3 rounded tbs. mango
½ lb. tomatoes	chutney
1 heaped tbs. plain flour	1 heaped tsp. salt
1 level tbs. turmeric	¼ tsp. pepper
powder	1 large can soya beans in
	tomato sauce

Trim roots and leaves off leeks, and discard. Clean leeks thoroughly by slitting lengthways down one side and washing under running water. Cut into pieces. Wash cauliflower and divide into pieces. Skin and slice onions. Peel, core and chop apple. Cut potatoes into equal pieces. Wash and chop tomatoes. Mix flour and turmeric in a large bowl. Toss vegetables and fruits in this. Heat fat in pan, toss in vegetables and fry lightly. Add curry powder, water, coriander seed and chutney. Cook for 30 mins. Add soya beans and heat through. Season to taste. Serve with boiled rice and green salad. Follow with a light sweet.

Rice

6 oz. brown rice
1 dessertsp. vegetable oil
water

Wash and pick over the rice. Put into a pan with the oil and well cover with water, bringing the level half as high again as the rice. Bring to the boil, put the lid on the pan and simmer for 20 mins. Strain off any remaining water.

Oranges

4 oranges
1 tbs. clear honey
3 dessertsp. warm water

4 tsp. almond cream or
whipped dairy cream
glacé cherries (optional)

Peel the oranges thinly and slice. Divide the slices between four dishes. Dissolve the honey in the water and pour over the oranges. Top with nut cream or whipped dairy cream, and decorate with glacé cherries if liked.

Menu 22

Shepherd's Pie

2 large onions
2 large carrots
2 oz. margarine
1 tsp. mixed herbs

4 tomatoes
1 large can Meatless Steaks
1 small can Nuttolene
1 lb. creamy mashed potatoes

Peel and chop the onions and peel and coarsely grate the carrots. Fry both in the margarine with the mixed herbs until tender. Add the tomatoes cut into small pieces. Drain the gravy off the Meatless Steaks, and put both Steaks and Nuttolene through the mincer. Add to the onion mixture, with the gravy. A little Marmite or Yeastrel may be added if desired, with extra water or stock if the mixture is too stiff. Place the whole in a fire-proof dish, cover carefully with the creamed potatoes, starting at the edges. Smooth with a fork, and put in the top of a hot oven, 450° F., gas mark 8, or under the grill, until the potato is browned.

Apple Fritters

4 oz. plain flour	¼ pint milk
1 heaped tsp. baking powder	1 tsp. cooking oil
1 egg	4 medium-sized cooking apples

Mix together the flour and baking powder, beat in the egg and gradually add the milk and oil. Peel and core the apples and cut them into ½" rounds. Dip them in the batter and fry until golden brown. Serve sprinkled with caster sugar

Menu 23

Mushroom Roll

8 oz. shortcrust pastry	1 small can Nuttolene or 12 oz. left over nutmeat
1 onion	
1 oz. margarine	3 tbs. sweet chutney
4 oz. mushrooms	salt and pepper

Make the pastry using 8 oz. plain wholemeal flour, 4 oz. vegetable fat, 2 teaspoonfuls baking powder, (or 12 oz. 'rubbed-in mixture') 2 tablespoonfuls cold water. Roll the shortcrust into a large oval. Peel, chop and fry the onion, and when tender, add the washed and chopped mushrooms. Cook for a further 5 mins. Cut the Nuttolene or nutmeat into small pieces. Mix all the ingredients together, season well. Place the mushroom mixture on one half of the pastry and fold over to form a crescent shape. If the edges of the pastry are first moistened, the two sides will stick together. Press down, brush with egg yolk (if following with apple meringue, use the egg yolk from this) and bake in a hot oven, 375° F., gas mark 5, for 15 mins. Serve with brown gravy (see page 48) and follow with a light protein-rich sweet.

Apple Meringue*

1½ lbs. apples	1 tsp. grated lemon rind
2 tbs. water	2 egg whites
1 tbs. honey or brown sugar	4 oz. caster sugar

Peel, core and quarter the apples and cook in ¼ pint of water until soft. Mash, sieve or liquidise. Add lemon rind and sweeten to taste. Put into an ovenproof dish. Beat the egg whites until stiff and dry, fold in the sugar, pile on top of the apple, spreading to the very edges of the dish, to seal, and bake at 275° F., gas mark 1, for 1½ hours until the meringue is crisp. (If following the mushroom roll as suggested, make apple meringue first, then remove from oven and increase heat to cook mushroom roll, putting the apple meringue under the grill or in the hot cupboard.)

Menu 24

Jacket Potato Boats

4 large potatoes	pinch cayenne
1 oz. butter	¼ pint milk
6 oz. grated cheese	salt and pepper

73

Scrub potatoes, score them horizontally round the middle, and bake in a hot oven 450° F., gas mark 8, for 1 hour or until tender. Cut around the score marks and pull apart. Scoop out the potato flesh, mash it well, add the butter, cheese, a pinch cayenne, ¼ pint creamy milk, salt and pepper, pile back into the skins, brown under a hot grill, or put back in the oven for 20 mins. until browned. Serve with carrots, leeks, or cauliflower in a white sauce.

Fruit Pie

8 oz. shortcrust pastry	2 oz. sugar
½ lb. apricots (soaked overnight) or 1½ lbs. apples or rhubarb (as in season)	4 tbs. water

Make the pastry using 8 oz. plain wholemeal flour, 4 oz. vegetable fat, 2 teaspoonfuls baking powder (or 12 oz. 'rubbed in mixture') and 2 tablespoonfuls cold water. Roll out thinly and line a pie tin with half of it. Put layers of apricots, or other fruit, prepared but not cooked, and sugar, ending with fruit. Pour the water over the fruit. Cover with the other half of the pastry. Bake in hot oven, 450° F., gas mark 8, for 10 mins., then turn down to 300° F., gas mark 2, and cook for a further 30 mins. Dredge with sugar and serve with cream or custard.

Menu 25

Nut Rissoles

2 oz. margarine	2 eggs
1 small onion	8 oz. milled almonds, hazel
1 stick celery or	nuts or walnuts
½ tsp. celery seed	½ tsp. Marmite (optional)
1 tsp. mixed herbs	salt and pepper
1 tbs. plain flour	4 oz. fresh breadcrumbs
¼ pint milk	toasted crumbs

Gently cook the chopped onion and celery or celery seed and mixed herbs in the margarine. Add the flour, stir well, add the milk, Marmite, one egg, nuts and crumbs, stir well and cook for 5 mins. Season to taste. Make into round shapes, coat in egg and breadcrumbs, and fry in shallow fat on top of the stove or in a moderate oven. Serve with brown gravy (see Menu 1, page 48).

Chocolate Pudding

4 oz. plain flour	4 oz. golden syrup
1 oz. cocoa	1 tsp. bicarbonate of soda
4 oz. vegetable shortening	$\frac{1}{4}$ pint milk

Mix together flour, cocoa, shortening and syrup. Dissolve bicarbonate of soda in the milk and mix quickly with the chocolate mixture. Put into a greased basin and steam for $1\frac{1}{2}$ hours. Turn out, sprinkle with caster sugar, and serve with custard, cream or top milk.

Menu 26

Baked Cheese Soufflé Pudding

6 oz. grated cheese	salt and pepper
1 clove chopped garlic (optional)	3 eggs, separated
4 oz. soft brown breadcrumbs	$\frac{1}{2}$ pint milk
pinch cayenne	2 oz. butter, melted

Mix all the dry ingredients together and add the well-beaten egg yolks, milk and melted butter. Beat the egg whites until a stiff froth. Fold this into the other ingredients; put the mixture into a greased soufflé dish, and bake in a moderate oven 425° F., gas mark 7, for 30 mins. Serve with onion sauce.

Onion Sauce

1 large onion	$\frac{1}{2}$ pint milk
1 oz. butter	salt and pepper
1 dessertsp. plain flour	nutmeg

Chop onions very finely and fry lightly in the butter for 10 mins., but do not brown. Add the flour, stir well, and add the milk very slowly. Cook gently for 20 mins., adding salt, pepper and nutmeg to taste. (Take care that the sauce does not catch the bottom of the pan when it thickens. A double saucepan helps to prevent this.)

Baked Apples

4 large apples	2 tbs. desiccated coconut
cooking dates	pinch cinnamon

Wash and core the apples and score skin round the middle. Stuff with a mixture of dates and coconut, and a pinch of cinnamon. Bake in a moderate oven, 375° F., gas mark 5, for 40 to 50 mins., until tender. Serve with cream.

Menu 27

Nuttolene Fritters

1 large can Nuttolene	½ tsp. rosemary (optional)
or other nutmeat	1 egg
4 oz. plain flour	¼ pint milk and water mixed
2 tsp. baking powder	salt and pepper

Open the can of Nuttolene at both ends and loosen the circular ends. Remove one circle, slip a knife round the edge of the Nuttolene to loosen it. Press it out of the can by pushing the remaining loose end. Cut it into thin slices. Make the batter by mixing all the other ingredients together and beating to a creamy consistency. Leave to stand for a time if possible. Dip the Nuttolene rounds in it and fry in hot fat. Serve with brown gravy (see Menu 1, page 48), braised tomatoes and other vegetable in season.

Banana Custard*

½ pint milk
2 eggs, beaten
1½ oz. sugar
¼ tsp. vanilla essence
¼ tsp. almond essence

4 bananas (or strawberries or
   raspberries or other fruit
   in season)
2 oz. dates, chopped
desiccated coconut

To make the custard, scald the milk, pour over the beaten eggs, return to the pan with the sugar and re-heat gently until the mixture thickens (do not let it boil), stirring all the time. Remove from heat and add essences. Peel and chop the bananas. Mix with the dates and divide between four glasses. (Omit dates if using raspberries or strawberries.) Pour the custard over the fruit, sprinkle with desiccated coconut and allow to cool. Top with whipped cream if desired.

Menu 28

Cashew Nut and Tomato Risotto

4 oz. brown rice
1 14-oz. can tomatoes
4 oz. grated cashew nuts
2 eggs, hardboiled
2 tbs. fresh chopped parsley
   or 1 tsp. dried parsley

grated rind and juice
   of ½ lemon
salt and freshly ground
   black pepper
cornflakes or whole-
   wheat flakes
butter
grated cheese

Wash the rice well. Put it into a pan and cover with cold water. Cook the rice for about 20 mins., adding more water if necessary. When it is tender, drain off all the water and mash in the tomatoes. Add the cashew nuts, chopped hardboiled eggs, parsley, lemon rind and juice. Season carefully with plenty of freshly ground black pepper and salt. Turn the mixture into a fireproof dish, cover the top with cornflakes and dabs of butter, and a scattering of grated cheese, and bake in a cool oven, 300° F., gas mark 2, for 20 mins. Or keep the mixture hot over the hotplate and just brown off the cornflakes under a hot grill before serving. Serve with a green vegetable.

Fruit Salad

2 bananas	1 medium-size can pineapple pieces
2 dessert apples	a few strawberries, raspberries, or
2 oranges	grapes, when available

Peel and chop the bananas, chop apples but do not peel, and squeeze orange juice over them. Drain syrup from the pineapple, and mix all fruits together.

Vegetables

GENERAL RULES FOR COOKING VEGETABLES

1. Always use as much of the vegetable as possible; peel or pare very thinly where necessary. The leaves of many vegetables, such as celery, cauliflower and turnips can be used, and contain much goodness.

2. Always cook for the minimum amount of time in the minimum amount of water, with the lid on the pan.

3. Never add bicarbonate of soda.

4. For everyday cooking a steamer (consisting of a pan with a strainer and lid) is invaluable. An assortment of different root vegetables, such as potatoes and carrots, also cauliflower, (added later), can be put together in the top part, and then greens or peas can be put in the bottom later and cooked for a very short time. Thus both heat and space on the stove are saved; you do not have to drain the vegetables in the top, and you can also place plates on top of the steamer instead of the lid, thus warming them at the same time; or you can keep food hot between a warm plate and the lid of the steamer.

5. Always drain all the water from vegetables and save it for use in gravy or soups, and toss the vegetables with a knob of butter or margarine and seasoning.

6. Remember when using frozen vegetables that they have already been partially cooked, and so need very little cooking. We find the nicest way of doing them is to let them thaw out completely and then just to toss them in butter over a very gentle heat for as long as is necessary to make them tender, and then to add seasoning.

The following are our favourite ways of cooking the common vegetables:

JERUSALEM ARTICHOKES, BAKED

1 or 2 artichokes per person. Scrub but do not peel. Place on a baking sheet with 2 oz. vegetable fat and bake in a moderately hot oven for 45 to 60 mins. until tender. Serve sprinkled with salt.

JERUSALEM ARTICHOKES, BOILED

Peel 1–1½ lbs. artichokes thinly and cut into thick slices. Put straight into water to prevent discoloration. Cook until tender just covered with water or in a steamer; drain off all the water, add 1 oz. butter, salt and freshly ground black pepper, 1 tablespoonful lemon juice and a little chopped parsley if available.

JERUSALEM ARTICHOKES, CREAMED

Prepare and cook as above, but when tender mash with 1 oz. butter and 2 tablespoonfuls top milk or cream, seasoning with salt, a squeeze of lemon juice and black pepper.

JERUSALEM ARTICHOKE FRITTERS

Peel 1–1½ lbs. artichokes thinly and cut into thick slices. Put straight into water to prevent discoloration. Cook as above, drain off all the water, and sprinkle the artichokes with a little chopped fresh or dried tarragon and a squeeze of lemon juice. Roll them in egg and bread-crumbs and fry until golden and crisp.

JERUSALEM ARTICHOKES IN CHEESE SAUCE

Useful as an extra source of protein in the main meal. Prepare and cook as above, and when tender drain and serve in cheese sauce (see page 94).

BROAD BEANS

Allow 2 lbs. of tender beans for 4 people, or about 4 lbs. of older ones. If the pods are young and tender, they need not be removed. Prepare by washing, topping and tailing and cutting into 1″ lengths. Otherwise shell and wash the beans. Put beans into enough fast boiling water to *barely* cover them and cook for 15 to 20 mins. with the lid on the pan until the beans are just tender. Strain, and add 1 oz. butter and 1 tablespoonful chopped fresh summer savoury or parsley, and season with salt and pepper. Alternatively, they may be served in a parsley or white sauce (see page 94).

FRENCH BEANS

Allow 2 lbs. beans for 4 people. Remove tough strings, top and tail and wash the beans. If longer than about 4″, cut into pieces. Put into enough boiling water to barely cover and cook with the lid on the pan for 10 to 15 mins. until tender. Strain off water and add 1 oz. butter, a good squeeze of lemon juice and salt and pepper. A little chopped fresh summer savoury or a teaspoonful of dried summer savoury is delicious with these if available.

RUNNER BEANS

Remove strings, top and tail and slice diagonally into 2″ lengths. Cook and season in the same way as French beans.

BEETROOT

Allow $1\frac{1}{2}$ lbs. for 4 people. Tiny beetroot are best if available. They may be bought already cooked, or prepared in the following way. Cut the leaves from the beetroot, not too near the root. Do not peel or cut off any root. Cover with water and simmer gently until tender. This may take up to 2 hours, depending on the size and age of the beetroot, but the process can be speeded up with the aid of a pressure cooker. Rub off the skins, and cut the beetroot into even-sized pieces if necessary. Toss in melted butter, sprinkle with a little sugar, salt and lemon juice or cider vinegar, and serve hot.

BEETROOT IN WHITE SAUCE

Prepare and cook as above, remove skins, cut beetroot into even-sized pieces and serve in a white sauce (see page 94).

CABBAGE

Allow 2 lbs. cabbage for 4 people.

With apple: wash and shred cabbage. Peel and chop 1 small cooking apple. Put into $\frac{1}{4}$" fast boiling water and cook for 5 mins. Strain, add 1 oz. butter, nutmeg, sugar and salt to taste. Red cabbage is delicious cooked in this way.

With caraway seeds and onion: wash and shred cabbage. Heat 2 tablespoonfuls corn oil in a pan; add $\frac{1}{2}$ teaspoonful caraway seeds and 1 small chopped onion, cook in the oil for 10 mins. but do not brown. Toss cabbage in the oil, cook over a very gentle heat for 2 to 5 mins., or until tender. Season with salt and pepper and serve immediately. (Caraway seeds can be omitted and a little more onion added if preferred.)

With tomato: wash and shred cabbage. Heat 1 cupful tomato juice and 1 teaspoonful sugar in a pan, add cabbage, a small clove garlic chopped, and a pinch of basil or dill. Cook cabbage until tender (2 to 5 mins.), add $\frac{1}{2}$ oz butter, salt and pepper to taste, and serve at once.

CARROTS, BOILED

Allow $1-1\frac{1}{2}$ lbs. carrots for 4 people. Scrape or peel thinly and if the carrots are large, cut into rings or fingers, or grate coarsely. Cook in enough fast boiling water to just cover, and cook until tender, (or steam until tender). Strain off water and add 1 oz. butter or margarine, salt, pepper and lemon juice to taste.

CARROTS, CREAMED

Scrape or peel thinly, cut into even-sized pieces and cook as above until tender. Strain off water, mash well and add 1 oz. butter or margarine, 2 tablespoonfuls top milk or cream, and salt, pepper and nutmeg to taste, (A mixture of turnips or swedes and carrots cooked in this way is also pleasant.)

CARROTS WITH PARSLEY

Prepare and cook as for boiled carrots. Strain off all water, add 1 oz. butter or margarine, $\frac{1}{2}$ teaspoonful sugar, salt and pepper to taste, and 1–2 tablespoonfuls chopped parsley. Toss well.

CAULIFLOWER

Wash the cauliflower thoroughly in salted water. Remove tough leaves but reserve tender ones and chop finely. Break cauliflower into florets and steam or cook in $\frac{1}{2}$" boiling water with the lid on the pan until just tender (5 to 10 mins. boiling, 10 to 15 mins. steaming). Strain off all water, add 1 oz. margarine or butter, salt and pepper and toss well.

CAULIFLOWER IN CHEESE SAUCE

Prepare and cook as above, drain well and serve in a cheese sauce (see page 94).

CELERY

Allow 1 good-sized stick of celery per person. Chop the sticks of celery, including the leaves, and put into a pan or casserole. If liked, add 1 teaspoonful coriander seed (wrapped in muslin), cover with water and cook until tender – about $\frac{3}{4}$ hour in the oven at 375° F., gas mark 5, or for 30 mins. on top of the stove.

CELERY IN CHEESE SAUCE

Prepare and cook as above, but drain off all the water and serve in a cheese sauce (see page 94).

CUCUMBER

Peel the cucumber, cut into $\frac{1}{2}$" rounds and cook in $\frac{1}{8}$" fast boiling water with the lid on the pan until tender – about 5 mins. Strain off all the water, add $\frac{1}{2}$ oz. butter or margarine and $\frac{1}{2}$ teaspoonful dill.

CUCUMBER, BRAISED

Prepare the cucumber as above. Put into an oven-proof dish and just cover with a mixture of milk and water. Put little pieces of butter on top and sprinkle with salt and pepper. Cover and cook in a moderate oven until tender – about 15 mins.

CUCUMBER IN CHEESE SAUCE

Prepare and cook as above, strain off all the water and serve in a cheese sauce (see page 94).

GREENS

Kale, spring greens, purple sprouting broccoli, white sprouting broccoli, the green part of cauliflowers can all be cooked in this way. Allow 2 lbs. greens for 4 people. Wash the greens thoroughly in salted water. Remove and discard tough parts and chop remainder. Cook quickly in about $\frac{1}{4}$" fast boiling water with the lid on the pan until tender, 2 to 5 mins., depending on the freshness of the vegetables. Drain off all the water, add 1 oz. butter or margarine, salt, pepper and a little celery seed or pinch nutmeg if desired.

GREENS IN CREAMY SAUCE

Prepare and cook as above, strain off all the water and serve in a white sauce (see page 94).

LEEKS

Allow 2 lbs. for 4 people. Trim off and discard roots and dark green leaves. Slit in half lengthwise and wash thoroughly under the tap. Cut into 2″ lengths, cook in a little boiling water with the lid on the pan until tender, 5 to 10 mins. Strain off all the water and add 1 oz. butter or margarine and a little chopped parsley if available.

LEEKS IN WHITE SAUCE

Prepare and cook as above, strain and serve in a white sauce (see page 94).

MARROW, BRAISED

Wash the marrow and remove pips and skin if tough. Cut into circles and place with a bay leaf and a pinch of coriander seed in an ovenproof dish. Pour over ½ cupful of milk and water, sprinkle with salt and pepper and a few pieces of butter. Bake in a moderate oven until tender, 20 to 30 mins.

MARROW IN CHEESE SAUCE

Prepare as above and cook with a bay leaf in ¼″ fast boiling water with the lid on the pan for about 5 mins. until tender, or use a steamer. Strain off all the water and serve in a cheese sauce (see page 94).

MARROW, STEWED

Prepare as for braised marrow and cut into ½″ dice.

Melt 2 oz. butter in a pan, add marrow, 1 bay leaf and a pinch of coriander seed if liked. Cook over a very gentle heat (with no water) for 10 to 15 mins. until the marrow is just tender.

MUSHROOMS, FRIED

Wash mushrooms but do not peel. Trim stems and cut into pieces if required. Cook gently in butter until tender. Add a little lemon juice if desired.

MUSHROOMS, GRILLED

Choose medium to large mushrooms. Wash and remove stalks. Lay mushrooms dark side uppermost on a baking dish. Put a piece of butter or a drop of cooking oil in the centre of each and season with salt and pepper. Cook under a grill or in a moderate oven until tender (about 20 mins.). Squeeze a little lemon juice over each mushroom before serving.

MUSHROOMS IN WHITE SAUCE

Cook as described for fried mushrooms and serve in a white sauce (see page 94).

Allow 1 lb. mushrooms for 4 people.

ONIONS, BAKED

Allow 1 good-sized onion per person. Wash onions but do not remove skins. Trim root end. Place on a baking sheet and bake in a moderately hot oven until tender (about 1 hour). Serve split, with butter.

ONIONS, BOILED

Remove skins and cut onions into quarters; stick a clove into each quarter and cook in $\frac{1}{2}''$ of fast boiling water with the lid on the pan for about 15 mins. until tender. Strain off water, add $\frac{1}{2}$ oz. butter or margarine, and salt and pepper to taste.

ONIONS, BRAISED

Prepare as above and cut into halves. Stick a clove in each half, put into an ovenproof dish and cover with milk and water. Sprinkle with salt, pepper and pieces of butter, and bake in a moderate oven until tender (about 30 to 40 mins.).

ONION RINGS, FRIED

Peel and cut into rings. Dip in milk and then in wholemeal flour. Fry in shallow fat until golden brown and crisp.

ONIONS IN SAUCE

Skin and chop onions, cook in $\frac{1}{2}$" boiling water with the lid on the pan until tender. Strain, and serve in a cheese or white sauce (see page 94).

PARSNIPS

Allow $1-1\frac{1}{2}$ lbs. for 4 people. Wash and peel thinly. Cut into even-sized pieces. Put in enough boiling water to just cover, cook with the lid on the pan, or steam until tender. Strain off the water, add 1 oz. butter, a little chopped parsley and a pinch of paprika pepper.

PARSNIPS, CREAMED

Prepare and cook as above. When tender, strain and mash. Add 1 oz. butter or margarine, 2 tablespoonfuls top milk or cream, and salt, pepper and nutmeg to taste.

PARSNIPS, FRIED

Prepare and cook as above, strain well. Sprinkle with salt and cayenne pepper. Roll in flour, dip in beaten egg and then roll in dried crumbs. Fry in hot vegetable fat until golden. Serve with slices of lemon.

PARSNIPS, ROAST

Prepare as above and parboil for 5 mins. Heat 2 oz. vegetable fat in a tin in the oven, then place the parsnips in this and baste well. Cook in a moderately hot oven until golden and crisp (about 45 mins.)

PEAS

Allow 2 lbs. peas for 4 people. If peas are the special 'sugar' variety, they may be washed and cooked in the pod. Otherwise, remove pods and wash peas. Cook in $\frac{1}{4}''$ fast boiling water with 1 teaspoonful sugar and a sprig of mint and the lid on the pan until just tender. Strain, add a knob of butter and some chopped parsley.

PEAS WITH LETTUCE

Prepare and cook as above, strain off all water and add 1 oz. butter. Chop one lettuce (or the equivalent in outside leaves) and add to the peas with 1 tablespoonful chopped mint. Toss well and cook gently for 2 mins.

POTATOES, BAKED

Choose even sized potatoes, allowing one per person. Scrub and prick with a fork. Place on a baking sheet and cook for about 1 hour at 400° F., gas mark 6, or until tender – this will depend on the size and type of the potatoes. Large new potatoes cook much more quickly than old ones. Serve split, with butter.

POTATOES, BOILED

Allow $\frac{1}{2}$ lb. for each person. Scrape or peel thinly, cut into equal-sized pieces (say half or quarter the potato if large), and place in cold water to prevent discoloration. Cover with cold water and cook for 20 to 30 mins. until tender, or cook in a steamer, allowing a little extra time. Strain off all the water and add 1 oz. butter or margarine, salt and pepper, and chopped parsley or mint when available, and shake lightly in the pan.

POTATOES, BOILED IN SKINS

Scrub potatoes and boil or steam in their skins until

tender. 1 teaspoonful of dill may be added to the water. Strain, and serve split, with butter, and sprinkled with salt.

POTATO CAKES

Roll small pieces of creamed potatoes in wholemeal flour and fry in shallow fat until browned on both sides. Drain off all fat on kitchen paper.

POTATOES, CHIPPED

Peel potatoes and cut into strips. Put into water to prevent discoloration. When ready to cook, blot off all water on an old clean cloth. Heat fat; if a test chip goes brown, it is too hot; if chip just sizzles and rises, fat is the right temperature. Plunge potatoes into the fat and cook until just soft but not brown. (Care is needed here. If too many chips are put in at once, the fat will bubble up and over.) Remove chips and drain. Re-heat fat until very hot, plunge the chips back for just a minute or two until browned. Drain and serve.

POTATOES, CREAMED

Prepare and cook as for boiled potatoes. Drain off all water and mash thoroughly. Add 1 oz. butter, 2 tablespoonfuls cream or top milk, salt, pepper and nutmeg to taste, and beat with a wooden spoon until very white and creamy.

POTATOES, DUCHESSE

Prepare and cook as for creamed potatoes but substituting one egg yolk for the milk or cream. The mixture should be fairly stiff. Put little heaps of potato on to a greased baking sheet and rough-up with a fork, or use a large piping bag and a $\frac{1}{2}''$ star nozzle. Bake in a moderate oven, 425° F., gas mark 7, until browned.

POTATOES, HUNGARIAN

Scrub medium-sized potatoes, but do not peel. Cut in half lengthwise and place cut-side down on a thickly greased baking sheet. Cook in a moderately hot oven for ½ to 1 hour until tender (this will depend on size and type of potato). The top will be soft and the bottom will be crisp like a roast potato. These can be left prepared in the oven for some hours previous to cooking in an automatic oven.

POTATOES, NEW

Scrub or scrape, and cook in sufficient boiling water to cover, adding 1 teaspoonful sugar and a sprig of mint, for about 20 mins., with the lid on the pan, until tender. Drain off all the water, add 1 oz. butter or margarine, and a little salt and pepper.

POTATOES, NEW, WITH PARSLEY

Prepare and cook as above. Drain off all water, add 1 oz. butter or margarine and 2–3 tablespoonfuls chopped parsley, and shake until well coated.

POTATOES, ROAST

Parboil peeled potatoes for 5 mins. Heat 2 oz. vegetable fat or oil in a tin in the oven, add well-drained potatoes, baste well and cook in the top of a hot oven for 45 to 60 mins. until golden and crisp. Drain on kitchen paper and serve lightly sprinkled with salt.

POTATOES, SAUTÉ

Scrape or thinly peel potatoes and cut into small even-sized pieces or grate coarsely. Heat 2 oz. fat in a pan, and toss potatoes in this. Cook gently, with the lid on the pan for 15 to 20 mins., until potatoes are tender, shaking the pan from time to time. Serve lightly sprinkled with salt.

SALSIFY

Allow 1–1½ lbs. for 4 people. Wash and peel thinly. Cut into even-sized pieces and put straight into cold water to prevent discoloration. Cook just covered with boiling water with the lid on the pan, or steam until tender. Strain off all the water, add 1 oz. butter, a little chopped parsley and lemon juice.

SALSIFY, CREAMED

Prepare and cook as above. When tender, strain and mash. Add 1 oz. butter or margarine, 2 tablespoonfuls top milk or cream, and salt, pepper and lemon juice to taste.

SALSIFY, FRIED

Prepare and cook as above, strain well. Sprinkle with salt and lemon juice. Roll in flour, dip in beaten egg and then roll in dried crumbs. Fry in hot fat until golden. Serve with slices of lemon.

SALSIFY IN WHITE SAUCE

Prepare and cook as above. Strain and serve in a white sauce (see page 94).

SPINACH

Allow 2 lbs. of spinach for 4 people. Wash thoroughly in plenty of cold running water. Remove any tough leaves. Discard tough stems but finely chop any tender ones and put into ⅛″ fast boiling water and cook for 2 mins., then add the spinach leaves. Put the lid on the pan and cook quickly until tender (2 to 5 mins.). Drain well, add 1 oz. margarine or butter, salt and a pinch of nutmeg. (Outside leaves of lettuce may also be cooked in this way.)

SPINACH, CREAMED

Prepare and cook as above. Drain well, add ½ oz. butter or margarine and beat thoroughly. Stir in 2 tablespoonfuls top milk or cream, salt and nutmeg to taste and serve immediately.

SPINACH IN CREAMY SAUCE

Prepare and cook as above. Drain well, and serve in a white sauce (see page 94).

SPROUTS

Allow 2 lbs. of sprouts for 4 people. Wash, remove any yellow or tough leaves and cut each sprout into two or four pieces, depending on size. Cook in about ¼″ fast boiling water for 2 to 5 mins., drain thoroughly, add a good knob margarine or butter, salt and pepper or celery salt and 1 tbs. chopped chives or parsley when available.

SPROUTS, STEWED

Prepare the sprouts as above and cut into quarters or eighths, depending on size. Melt 2 oz. margarine in a pan and toss in the sprouts. Put the lid on the pan, and cook over a very gentle heat until just tender (5 to 10 mins.), shaking the pan from time to time. Season with salt, pepper and a little celery seed if liked, and add fresh chopped parsley or chives when available.

SWEDES

Allow 1½ lbs. for 4 people. Peel thinly and cut into even-sized pieces. Cover with water and cook with the lid on the pan until tender. Strain off water and add 1 oz. butter or margarine, salt, pepper and nutmeg to taste, and a little chopped parsley when available.

SWEDES, CREAMED

Prepare and cook as above. Strain off all water, mash well and add 1 oz. butter or margarine, 2 tablespoonfuls top milk or cream, and salt, pepper and nutmeg to taste.

SWEDES, CREAMED WITH CARROTS

Prepare and cook a mixture of half swedes, half carrots. When tender drain off all water, mash well and add 1 oz. butter or margarine, 2 tablespoonfuls top milk or cream, and salt, pepper and nutmeg to taste.

SWEET CORN ON THE COB

Remove husks and silky threads from the cob and cook in boiling water for about 20 mins. until tender. Do not cook too long or too fast or the corn will begin to harden again. Strain the water, toss in plenty of butter and season with salt and pepper.

SWEET CORN, BUTTERED

Prepare and cook as for corn on the cob, strain, and, using a fork, scrape the corn from the cob, or use strained, canned sweet corn. Add 1 oz. butter, salt and pepper to taste and serve piping hot.

SWEET CORN IN CHEESE SAUCE

Prepare and cook as above, or use strained, canned sweet corn and serve in a cheese sauce (see page 94).

TOMATOES

Wash tomatoes and remove their stalks. Cut in half horizontally, sprinkle with a little sugar and a little salt, freshly ground black pepper and a pinch of basil. Top with a small dab of butter or margarine and cook in a moderate oven or under a moderate grill until the butter has melted and the tomatoes are lightly cooked.

TOMATOES, CANNED

To a small can of tomatoes add 1 teaspoonful sugar, salt and pepper, a pinch basil and a pinch dill, and heat gently.

TOMATOES WITH ONIONS

Allow half tomatoes, half onions. Peel and chop onions and cook gently in 2 oz. margarine until tender. Add peeled and quartered tomatoes and stir well. Season with salt and pepper, and sprinkle with chopped parsley if available.

TURNIPS

Allow 1½ lbs. of turnips for 4 people. Tiny turnips are best if available. Peel thinly and cut into even-sized pieces if they are big. Cook just covered with boiling water with the lid on the pan until tender. Strain off all the water, add 1 oz. butter or margarine, salt and pepper and chopped parsley if available.

TURNIPS, CREAMED

Prepare and cook as above. When tender, strain off all the water and mash well, or put through the mouli. Add 1 oz. butter or margarine, 2 tablespoonfuls top milk or cream, and salt and pepper to taste.

TURNIPS IN CHEESE SAUCE

Prepare and cook as above. When tender, strain well and serve in a cheese sauce (see page 94).

TURNIP TOPS

Allow 2 lbs. of turnip tops for 4 people. Wash turnip tops and cut small, removing tough stems. Cook for about 5 mins. in ¼″ water with the lid on the pan. Drain thoroughly and cover with parsley sauce (see page 94). adding a knob of butter and a pinch of nutmeg.

Any rather uninteresting green vegetables are delightful served in this way.

Sauces for Vegetables

Many of the vegetables previously described are enhanced by one of the following sauces:

White Sauce

1 oz. butter or margarine	salt
1 oz. cornflour	pepper
½ pint milk	

Melt the margarine, stir in the cornflour. Gradually beat in the milk and stir over a low heat until thickened. Season to taste.

This goes especially well with beetroot, broad beans, greens, leeks, mushrooms, onions, salsify, spinach.

Parsley Sauce

1 oz. margarine or butter	salt and pepper
1 oz. cornflour	1 tsp. grated lemon rind
½ pint milk	2 tbs. chopped parsley

Melt the margarine, stir in the cornflour. Gradually beat in the milk. Cook until thickened, stirring over a low heat. Season to taste and add chopped parsley and lemon rind.

This goes especially well with broad beans, celery, leeks, turnip tops.

Cheese Sauce

1 oz. margarine	2 oz. grated cheese
1 oz. wholemeal flour	salt and cayenne pepper
½ pint milk	

Melt the margarine and stir in the flour; gradually add the milk, stirring all the time over a low heat until thickened. Remove from heat, stir in cheese and season to taste.

This is a useful sauce to serve when additional protein is required in the meal and goes especially well with artichokes, cauliflower, celery, cucumber, marrow, onions, sweet corn, turnips.

V

QUICK MEALS

The meals in this section are for those occasions when you need to make a meal on the spur of the moment and have it on the table in 15 mins. to half an hour. They are all sustaining meals, and some of them are quite suitable for entertaining when unexpected guests arrive and you need something a little special. The recipes make use of canned, and packet foods, and it is helpful to keep an emergency shelf (preferably a high one so that it is not too often depleted by everyday use!) of these foods.

When making these meals we find it saves time to turn on both hot plates and put a pan with $\frac{1}{2}$" of water in it for the vegetables immediately before starting any of the preparations. We usually put the plates to warm on top of one of the pans.

If your store cupboard contains the following items you should be able to make any of the recipes in this chapter at a moment's notice:

EMERGENCY STORE

Canned Foods

Apple purée
Apricots
Butter beans
Carrots
Celery hearts
Cranberry sauce
Cream
Evaporated milk

Green beans
Grilling mushrooms
Nuttolene*
Peaches
Pears
Pineapple rings
Potatoes
Prunes
Rice pudding

Soya beans in tomato
    sauce*
Sweet corn
Tomatoes
Tomato juice

Packets

Birchermuesli*
Chocolate (raw sugar)*
Chocolate moulds*
Cornflakes (or whole-
    wheat* flakes)
Coconut (desiccated)
Dates
Digestive or sweetmeal*
    biscuits
'Instant' mashed potato*
Jellies (orange, lemon,
    blackcurrant)*
Nuts (grind a few extra
    when making savouries
    and keep in a jar for
    quick use)*
Sultanas

Flavourings

Bay leaves
Cider vinegar
Curry powder
Dry mustard

Garlic
Lemon juice
Mace (ground)
Marmite (or equivalent)
Mixed herbs
Nutmeg (grated)

Garnishes

Angelica or glacé pineapple
Blanched almonds
Chocolate sugar strands
Glacé cherries
Parsley
Walnuts

Perishables (bought fresh
    when needed and used
    with the above)

Bananas
Cauliflower
Eggs
Frozen vegetables
Leeks
Lemons
Mushrooms
Onions
Parsley
Tomatoes
Watercress

* Obtainable from Health Food Stores.

Menu 1

Vegetables in Cheese Sauce (10 mins.)

2 large packets mixed frozen vegetables	6 oz. grated cheese
2 oz. margarine	pinch dry mustard
2 oz. plain flour	salt and pepper
1 pint milk	4 tomatoes

Heat $\frac{1}{2}''$ water in a large pan, and when the water boils add the frozen vegetables and cook with the lid on until tender. Meanwhile make the cheese sauce by melting the margarine in a pan, draw aside the pan and stir in flour to a smooth paste. Add the milk, stir until thickened, then add the mustard and cheese and remove from heat. Drain frozen vegetables, and pour the cheese sauce over them. Serve garnished with a fresh tomato for each person, and plenty of watercress.

Prune whip

2 large cans prunes	1 tsp. orange rind
1 tin cream or $\frac{1}{4}$ pint double cream	4 blanched almonds

Drain the syrup from the prunes and pass them through a mouli. Whip cream and fold into prune purée. Grate in 1 teaspoonful orange rind, divide mixture between four dishes, and decorate with blanched almonds if available.

Menu 2

Quick Stew (15 mins.)

2 large onions	$\frac{1}{2}$ pint water or stock
2 oz. margarine	1 can tomatoes
1 small cabbage or large can green beans or packet frozen beans	1 can potatoes
	1 can carrots
	1 large can Nuttolene or other nutmeat
1 heaped tsp. mixed herbs	salt and pepper
1 bay leaf	2 tbs. chopped parsley if available
2 tbs. plain flour	

Chop the onions and cook in a large pan in the margarine for 5 mins., taking care not to let them get brown. Meanwhile wash and chop the cabbage (if using this), and add to the onions, tossing them together in the margarine; or drain off the water from the beans and add. Add the herbs, bay leaf and flour; stir well, then add the water, tomatoes, drained potatoes and carrots. Cut the Nuttolene into cubes, and add this. Cook for 5 mins. until all the vegetables are heated through. Season to taste, and sprinkle with chopped parsley if available. Serve with watercress, or other fresh green salad.

Apple Crumble

Start this before making the main part of the meal.

> 1 can apple purée
> 6 oz. 'rubbed-in' fat and flour, or
>   4 oz. plain flour and 2 oz. margarine
> 2 oz. brown sugar

Switch the oven to 350° F., gas mark 4. Put the apple into an ovenproof dish. Rub together the fat, flour and sugar until the 'breadcrumb' stage is reached. Pile this mixture on top of the apple and put into the oven. By the time the sweet stage of the meal is reached this will be cooked.

Menu 3

Potato and Soya Bean Fry (15 mins.)

1 large onion	2 large cans soya beans
4 large potatoes (uncooked)	in tomato sauce
2 oz. cooking fat or oil	2 tbs. chopped parsley

Chop the onion thinly; peel the potatoes and cut into ½″ cubes. Melt the fat in a large saucepan or deep-lidded frying pan; add the onions and potatoes and fry for 10 mins. with the lid on the pan, stirring occasionally. Meanwhile chop the parsley. Then tip in the soya beans and heat through. Garnish with the chopped parsley and serve with frozen vegetables.

Banana Flan

This takes a little longer to make, so it is a good idea to prepare it before starting on the savoury.

12 digestive biscuits	6 bananas
3 oz. butter	1 tbs. lemon juice
1 large can cream or	sugar to taste
¼ pint double cream	desiccated coconut

Crush biscuits between two sheets of greaseproof paper, using a rolling pin. Melt butter and stir into biscuit crumbs. Line pie dish with the mixture, and leave in a cool place while preparing the filling.

Whip the cream. Peel and mash the bananas with the lemon juice, then fold in the cream. Sweeten to taste and pile into the flan case. Sprinkle with desiccated coconut, and leave in a cool place until required.

Menu 4

Savoury Potato Cakes

1 lb. creamy mashed potatoes or 1 pkt. instant mashed potatoes and ½ pint milk	1 clove garlic (optional)
	4 oz. finely milled hazel nuts or grated cheese
1 oz. butter	salt and pepper

Use leftover mashed potatoes, or make them by cutting potatoes small and cooking in a pressure cooker and then straining them and mashing with butter and a little milk; or make up instant mashed potato according to instructions on packet. Chop garlic finely (if used) and fry lightly in the butter, then beat in the potato and the nuts, and season with salt and pepper. Form into cakes and roll lightly in flour. Fry in hot fat until crisp on both sides. Serve with fresh tomatoes and tossed green salad or frozen vegetables.

Tossed green salad

In a large bowl mix 1 tablespoonful cider vinegar, 3 tablespoonfuls olive oil, and a little salt and pepper. Add assorted chopped green vegetables in season, e.g. lettuce, endive, young spinach or cabbage leaves, cress, water-cress, celery leaves, chicory, and mix well. Serve at once.

Quick Apricot Jelly

If you make this jelly before starting to prepare the savoury part of the meal, and leave it in a cool place, it will be ready by the time the sweet stage of the meal is reached, because agar agar sets much more quickly than gelatine.

> $\frac{3}{4}$ pint water
> 1 lemon or orange vegetarian jelly
> 1 medium can apricots or peaches

Boil the water and pour over the jelly powder. Stir well. Drain the syrup from the fruit and place fruit on a shallow dish. Pour the jelly over and leave to set.

Menu 5

Leeks, Onions, or Cauliflower au Gratin

(15 mins.)

1 large cauliflower	2 oz. margarine
or	2 oz. plain flour
2 lbs. leeks	1 pint milk
or	6 oz. grated cheese
6 large onions	pinch dry mustard
	cornflakes

Put $\frac{1}{2}$″ water in a large pan and bring to boil. Prepare the cauliflower and break into florets; chop any tender green leaves; or prepare the leeks by cutting off tough green parts, trimming roots, slicing in half lengthwise, and washing thoroughly, then cutting into 1″ pieces; or peel and chop onions fairly finely. Cook in the boiling water until tender. Meanwhile make the sauce by melting the margarine in a large pan, and making a roux with the flour by stirring it into the melted fat till well mixed, then adding the milk and stirring until thickened. Remove from stove, and add cheese and mustard. Drain vegetables (save water for soups, etc.) and put them into an ovenproof dish. Cover with the cheese sauce and top with cornflakes, little pieces of margarine and a grating of cheese. Put under a hot grill until top is crisp. Serve with frozen green vegetables and canned potatoes which have been cut into slices and tossed in a little butter, then sprinkled with parsley.

Creamy Pears With Cranberry Sauce

1 medium can pears
1 large can rice pudding

1 small can cranberry sauce
  or some blackcurrant
  syrup

Drain the syrup from the pears. Divide the rice pudding between four dishes. Top each with a pear half, cut side down, and spoon the cranberry sauce, or blackcurrant syrup, on top of that, so that it runs down the pear attractively.

Menu 6

Portuguese Eggs (15 mins.)

6 eggs
2 oz. butter
1 small onion
4 tomatoes
2 oz. mushrooms (or 1
  small can)
2 heaped tbs. plain flour

1 pint milk
salt and pepper to taste
1 tbs. chopped parsley
1 tsp. grated lemon rind
1 tbs. lemon juice

Hardboil the eggs. Meanwhile melt the butter in a saucepan, add the finely chopped onion, the cut-up tomatoes and mushrooms, and cook for 10 mins. Add the flour, stir well; add the milk, bring to the boil and simmer for 10 mins. Add the parsley, lemon rind and juice, and salt and pepper to taste. Cut the eggs into quarters, arrange in a dish and pour the sauce over them. Serve very hot with a green vegetable and mashed potatoes cooked in the pressure cooker, or the 'instant' type.

Variations

Sprinkle dry breadcrumbs or cornflakes on top, dot with butter and grated cheese, and brown in the oven. Many different sauces can be used – curry, mushroom, celery, cheese, onion, asparagus, etc.

Blackcurrant Creams

1 blackcurrant jelly
¾ pint boiling water
1 small can evaporated milk

Empty the jelly powder into a measuring jug or bowl and pour the boiling water over it, stirring well. Allow to cool slightly, then stir in the evaporated milk. Pour into individual glasses and put aside to set. If this is prepared before starting on the main part of the meal, by the time the family has eaten the first course these creams will have set.

Menu 7

Cashew Nut and Celery Timbale (15 mins.)

1 onion
1 bay leaf
2 oz. margarine
1 can celery hearts
1 tbs. flour
1 can tomato juice

juice and rind of ½ lemon
6 oz. milled cashew nuts
1 tbs. parsley
pinch mace
salt and pepper

Chop the onion and cook with the bay leaf in margarine with the lid on the pan, until tender but not browned (10 mins.). Meanwhile open the can of celery hearts and chop into ½″ pieces. Add these to the onion mixture, then stir in the flour and tomato juice. Cook until slightly thickened, then stir in lemon rind and juice, cashew nuts, parsley and mace, and season with salt and pepper. Serve with fried canned potatoes and frozen green vegetables.

Quick Apple Fool

1 can apple purée	grated lemon rind
1 large can cream	angelica

Mix together the apple purée and cream, and grate in 1 tsp. lemon rind; add sugar or honey to taste, and serve decorated with a little chopped angelica and grated lemon rind.

Menu 8

Nutmeat Fricassée (15 mins.)

2 large onions	1 bay leaf
4 oz. mushrooms (or	2 oz. margarine
1 small can)	1 large can Nuttolene
1 small can tomatoes	salt and pepper

Peel and chop onions, wash and cut mushrooms into quarters. Cook the onions and mushrooms in the margarine with the bay leaf for 10 mins. Meanwhile open the can of Nuttolene and cut it into ½″ cubes. Add the tomatoes and Nuttolene to the onion mixture. Season well with salt and pepper. Serve immediately with fried canned potatoes and frozen spinach or peas.

Gay Bananas

1 banana per person
1 small can cream
chocolate sugar strands

Remove a piece of skin from the top of a banana about
½″ wide and the length of the banana. Pile or pipe a
whirl of cream along this slit and top with chocolate
sugar strands.

Menu 9

Butter Beans and Mushroom Savoury
(10 mins.)

2 large cans butter beans	1 can grilling mushrooms
2 oz. butter	or 4 oz. mushrooms
1 tbs. lemon juice	1 oz. grated cheese
salt and pepper to taste	1 oz. breadcrumbs

Put the butter beans through a mouli or liquidise them.
Heat them with the butter in a pan or flameproof
casserole dish. Add lemon juice, salt and pepper. Wash,
chop and fry mushrooms, if using fresh ones, or open the
can and drain off liquid. Add mushrooms to the butter
bean mixture, top with grated cheese and breadcrumbs,
and brown under a hot grill. Serve immediately with
mashed potatoes (quickly prepared in a pressure cooker,
or use the 'instant' type for a speedy meal) and frozen
green vegetables. Tomato chutney is delicious with this
savoury.

Instant Muesli

8 tbs. packet Bircher-muesli	fresh strawberries or raspberries when in season
milk	
cream if available	

Mix the muesli with enough milk to make a soft consistency. Put the mixture into individual glasses and top with cream and strawberries or raspberries when in season.

Menu 10

Cheese and Potato Pie (10 mins.)

1 lb. cooked mashed potatoes or 1 pkt. 'instant' potatoes and ½ pint milk	6 oz. grated cheese
	¼ tsp. nutmeg
	2 tomatoes
1 oz. butter	salt and pepper

If you have a pressure cooker cut 1 lb. potatoes into small pieces and cook until tender. Then strain, add butter and a little milk. Or, make up 'instant' mashed potato according to the instructions on the packet, using the milk and adding a good knob of butter. Add cheese, nutmeg, salt and pepper. Pile into a casserole dish, top with slices of tomato, and lightly brown under grill. Serve with frozen vegetables.

Stuffed Pears

8 pear halves (canned)
1 can cream
1 tbs. each of chopped glacé cherries, chopped walnuts or almonds, sultanas, chopped glacé pineapple or angelica

Drain syrup from fruit. Whip cream, fold in all the dried fruits and nuts, and pile into the centre of the fruit.

Menu 11

Nuttolene in Brown Gravy (10 mins.)

1 onion	1 tsp. Marmite
1 oz. vegetable fat	½ tsp. curry powder
1 tbs. plain flour	1 large can Nuttolene or other nutmeat
½ pint water	
	salt and pepper

Chop onion very finely and cook in the fat for 5 mins. Meanwhile open the can of Nuttolene and cut into chunks. Add flour to onion mixture and allow to brown. Add water and Marmite. Stir well and allow to thicken, then add curry powder, Nuttolene and salt and pepper. Cook for 5 mins. Serve with 'instant' mashed potatoes and frozen vegetables.

Canned Fruit

Drain syrup from a can of fruit (any variety). Divide fruit between four dishes and cover with freshly squeezed orange juice, and a few sultanas if liked. Serve with top milk.

Menu 12

Golden Fritters (15 mins.)

4 oz. plain flour	¼ pint milk or milk and water
pinch salt	1 tsp. oil; oil for frying
1 egg	1 12–oz. can sweet corn

Put the flour into a large bowl and mix in the salt and egg. Beat until blended, then add the milk and oil and beat again until smooth. Drain the sweet corn well and add to the batter mixture. Put tablespoonfuls of the mixture into hot fat and fry on both sides. Serve immediately with heated canned tomatoes and a green vegetable, with or without potatoes, and follow with a protein rich sweet, or biscuits and cheese.

Quick Chocolate Moulds

1 pkt. chocolate mould	1 small can evaporated milk
¾ pint milk	grated chocolate

If this is prepared before starting on the main part of the meal, by the time the family has eaten the first course these moulds will have set. Empty the mould into a saucepan and blend with half the milk. Bring to the boil, and cook for 1 min., stirring. Remove from heat and gradually stir in the rest of the milk and the evaporated milk. Pour into individual glasses and leave in a cool place to set. Decorate with coarsely-grated chocolate.

VI

ENTERTAINING

Although many vegetarians find that their diet gets simpler as time goes on and they learn to appreciate the delicate flavours of the fruits, nuts and vegetables in the diet, there are times when a more elaborate meal is required, and the recipes in this chapter have been found to meet such occasions.

We may sometimes feel a little hesitant about offering vegetarian dishes to meat-eating friends but we have found this is unnecessary, as such friends are inevitably intrigued and delighted – not to mention surprised – by the attractiveness of the food. It is perhaps wise to choose the recipe to suit particular guests – the special curry, mushroom nut flan, stuffed peppers, and the cheese fritters being particularly suitable for those totally unfamiliar with (or antagonistic to) vegetarian cooking.

Perhaps the key to successful entertaining lies in the advance preparation of the foods. The menus in this section have been planned to enable the hostess to prepare most of the items in advance, leaving her free to give her attention to her guests and to the finishing touches and attractive garnishes which will make her meal something special. We have given recipes for the first course, main dish and accompanying sauce or garnishes, and sweet course. Each menu has been carefully worked out to provide a balanced and varied meal, but of course different combinations of the various dishes can equally well be used.

It is a good idea to have the vegetables prepared and left in a cool place ready to cook at the last minute, or, easier still, to take advantage of the quickly-cooked frozen vegetables, but to transform them into something special by imaginative flavourings and garnishes, such as:

with peas – chopped fresh mint or parsley and butter.
    – butter and chopped raw lettuce.

with peas and carrots – finely chopped cooked onion and butter.

with broad beans – dried or chopped fresh summer savoury and butter.
    – parsley sauce.
    – white sauce flavoured with a little grated lemon rind and juice.
    – parsley, butter and a little lemon juice.

with runner or French beans – butter and dried or chopped fresh summer savoury.
    – butter, chopped fresh parsley and lemon juice.
    – butter and toasted almonds.

with brussel sprouts – butter and chopped fresh parsley.
    butter and chopped fresh chives.
    – butter, cooked chestnuts and chopped parsley.

with sweet corn – plenty of butter.
    – a little cream.

with broccoli spears – a quick mock hollandaise sauce made by adding 2 oz. butter, an egg yolk, and the juice of half a lemon to 1 pint of white sauce.

with spinach – butter and grated nutmeg.
    – cream and grated nutmeg.

It adds to the attractiveness if one can plan the colour of the meal carefully, choosing contrasting vegetables, such as carrots with spinach, or peas with braised tomatoes. If the main part of the meal is white it is attractively set off by dark vegetables, such as greens; if it is dark, light vegetables such as cauliflower or celery make a pleasant contrast. The use of garnishes, such as lemon halves or butterflies, thinly sliced tomatoes, chopped mint, fried mushrooms, toasted almonds, chives or parsley sprigs also add to the attractiveness of the meal.

For many people, a little wine enhances a dinner party and blends perfectly with vegetarian food. As a general rule, we find red wines particularly good with the darker nuts, such as walnuts, while white wine is delightful with the light coloured nuts, such as cashew nuts, and a rosé wine seems to harmonise with most dishes.

Finally, when serving-up it is a help to put all the dirty pans and cooking utensils straight into a bowl of hot, soapy water – this makes the unwelcome late-night or early-morning task of washing up so much easier!

Menu 1

Pineapple with Orange

1 large pineapple (or 1 large can pineapple chunks)	Fresh mint leaves or angelica Juice of 2 oranges

Peel the pineapple and chop into small chunks removing any hard pieces of core. If using canned pineapple, drain off all the syrup. Divide pineapple between dishes and cover with orange juice. Leave in a cool place until required, and serve garnished with fresh mint leaves or angelica. Hand round sugar if desired.

Nutmeat with Mushroom Stuffing

1 large onion	$\frac{1}{4}$ tsp. ground mace
2 oz. butter	$\frac{1}{4}$ tsp. nutmeg
1 level tsp. mixed herbs	2 oz. fresh breadcrumbs
1 heaped tbs. plain flour	juice and rind of $\frac{1}{2}$ lemon
$\frac{1}{4}$ pint milk	1 egg white
8 oz. grated cashew nuts, ground almonds or grated walnuts	salt and pepper

Peel and chop the onion and cook gently in the butter with the herbs for 10 mins. until soft but not browned. Add the flour and the milk and stir until thickened. Add the rest of the ingredients and mix well. Season to taste. Grease a pound loaf tin or casserole with butter and put in half the mixture, spread the stuffing, and then add the rest of the nut mixture. Cover with foil and bake in a moderate oven, 350° F., gas mark 4, for 1 hour. Turn out carefully on to a large plate and serve surrounded with roast potatoes and garnished with parsley and slices of lemon. This nutmeat can be prepared several hours beforehand and left in a cool place, covered with foil ready for baking.

Mushroom Stuffing

$\frac{1}{2}$ lb. mushrooms	6 oz. brown breadcrumbs
2 oz. butter	1 egg yolk
1 heaped tsp. Marmite	salt and pepper

Wash and roughly chop mushrooms and fry in the butter until tender – about 5 mins. Stir in all the other ingredients, season to taste. (Alternatively the recipe given for stuffing balls on page 124 can be used in the centre of the nutmeat, thus giving the classic poultry-stuffing flavour.)

Chocolate Ice-Cream Flan

6 oz. plain raw sugar
  chocolate
2 oz. butter or margarine
2 tbs. milk

5 oz. desiccated coconut
2 oz. icing sugar or brown
  sugar

Melt chocolate, fat and milk in a bowl over a saucepan of hot water. Remove bowl from heat and stir in the icing sugar or brown sugar and coconut. Press into a buttered dish and leave to set for about 2 hours. Fill with spoonsful of ice-cream.

Vanilla Ice-Cream

¼ pint milk
1½ oz. caster sugar
1 egg, beaten

¼ tsp. vanilla essence
¼ pint double cream

Make custard by heating together the milk and sugar and pour over the beaten egg. Return to the pan and cook over a low heat until thickened, stirring all the time. Stir in the vanilla essence and allow to cool. Whisk the cream lightly and strain in the custard. Place in freezing compartment of refrigerator for half an hour, then remove and whisk thoroughly. Return to freezer until frozen but still soft.

Menu 2

Tomatoes with Basil

8 fresh tomatoes
½ tsp. brown sugar
¼ tsp. salt
½ tsp. basil

freshly ground black pepper
3 tbs. olive or vegetable oil
1 tbs. cider vinegar
fresh parsley

Peel the tomatoes and cut into quarters or eighths depending on size. Sprinkle with sugar, salt, pepper and basil, and put into small dishes. Chill. At the last minute pour over a dressing made by shaking together in a screw-top jar the oil and cider vinegar. Sprinkle lavishly with chopped parsley (this may be chopped beforehand and left in a cool place until ready).

Asparagus and Almond Ring

1 medium onion	$\frac{1}{4}$ pint milk
2 oz. butter	1 egg
1 tsp. mixed herbs	salt and pepper
1 tbs. plain flour	8 oz. milled almonds
	4 oz. breadcrumbs

Peel and finely chop onion and cook with the mixed herbs in the butter until soft but not brown, about 10 mins. Blend in the flour, then add the milk, beaten egg and the rest of the ingredients and cook gently for 2 mins. Grease a large flat casserole dish or oven sheet, and place the almond mixture on it in the shape of a ring with a hole in the middle. Bake in a slow oven, 325° F., gas mark 3, for 1 hour. Remove from oven and place on serving dish. Fill the centre with the asparagus mixture and garnish with roasted almonds and fresh parsley sprigs. This ring may be cooked in advance and simply filled with stuffing and heated through in a warm oven when required.

Asparagus Stuffing

4 oz. button mushrooms	1 small can asparagus
2 oz. butter	salt and pepper
4 tomatoes	parsley

Wash the mushrooms and cook gently in the butter for 5 mins. Remove the skins from the tomatoes by immersing in boiling water for 1 min. and then plunging them into cold water. Cut the tomatoes into quarters and add to the mushrooms. Drain the water from the asparagus, cut each stick into three pieces, and add to the mushroom mixture. Keep over the heat until the tomatoes and asparagus have heated through, then season to taste and use to fill the almond ring as directed above, garnishing with fresh parsley. (Drain off excess liquid.)

Baked Alaska

1 wholemeal sponge cake (½ victoria sandwich mixture) or 3 small bought sponge cakes	2 egg whites 4 oz. caster sugar vanilla ice-cream (as in Menu 1) or 1 block vanilla ice-cream
1 small can pineapple pieces	

Put the sponge in the bottom of a fireproof dish and pour the pineapple pieces and their syrup over it. Leave in a cool place to allow syrup to soak into the sponge. It can be left for several hours.

Have the oven ready heated to 450° F., gas mark 8. Beat up the egg whites until really stiff and fold in the sugar. When ready to serve put the ice-cream on top of the sponge mixture, and spread the meringue on top of that, being careful to spread it right to the edges of the dish. Put into the oven for 1 min. until meringue has browned. Serve at once.

Vanilla Ice-Cream

See recipe given in Menu 1, p. 112.

Menu 3

Minted Grapefruit with Orange

2 oranges	1 drop of oil of peppermint (optional)
2 grapefruit	caster sugar to taste
4 sprigs fresh mint	

Peel the oranges and chop flesh into small pieces. Cut grapefruits in half and scoop out flesh. Chop finely, removing pips and pith. Mix oranges and grapefruit, add caster sugar to taste, and a drop of oil of peppermint.

Pile this mixture into grapefruit shells, and sprinkle with chopped fresh mint. Leave in a cool place until required.

Mushroom Nut Flan

1 small onion	1 tbs. plain flour
1 tsp. mixed herbs	¼ pint milk
½ tsp. celery seed (optional)	8 oz. grated almonds
	4 oz. breadcrumbs
2 oz. margarine	2 eggs
	salt and pepper

Chop onion finely and cook gently in the margarine with the herbs and celery seed until soft but not browned, about 10 mins. Blend in the flour and milk, stir well until thickened. Add rest of ingredients and salt and pepper to taste. Cook for 2 mins., then allow to cool. Spread into a greased oven-to-table pie dish, flattening the mixture round the base and sides to resemble pastry. Cook for 20 to 30 mins. in moderate oven, at 350° F., gas mark 4, until golden. Fill with mushroom mixture, and re-heat at 350° F., gas mark 4, for 10 mins. The 'flan' part of this dish can be prepared beforehand and left in a cool place for filling with the mushrooms and re-heating when required.

Mushroom Filling

1 small onion	2 tbs. plain flour
2 oz. butter	½ pint milk
8 oz. mushrooms	salt and pepper
½ tsp. marjoram	

Chop onion finely and cook in the butter with the washed and chopped mushrooms and herbs for 10 mins. Add the flour, stir well, add the milk and cook until thickened. Season to taste. Pour into the 'flan' as directed above.

Meringue Gâteau

2 egg whites	4 oz. granulated sugar
4 oz. caster sugar	¼ pint water
1 level dessertsp.	2 egg yolks
Nescafé	3 oz. plain raw sugar chocolate
4 oz. butter	1 oz. grated chocolate

Cover 2 upturned baking trays with kitchen foil. B
pressing down with a pan lid 6″ in diameter, mark
circles without tearing the foil. Grease the circles with o
or fat. Put oven to 175° F., or lowest gas setting. Mak
the meringue by beating the egg whites until really sti
and then folding in the caster sugar and Nescafé. Sprea
this mixture over the shapes on the foil and bake in a ver
slow oven for 3 hours or until thoroughly dried out. Allo
to cool, then carefully remove the meringue circles fro
the foil.

Meanwhile make the cream filling. Break the choc
late into pieces and put into a bowl over a pan of boilin
water to melt. Beat the butter until very light, beat in th
egg yolks and melted chocolate. Put granulated suga
and water into a pan and heat until the thread stage i
reached. To test this, put a little between finger an
thumb and draw them apart; if a thin thread form
between them the mixture is ready. Allow to cool slightl
then very gradually beat the sugar syrup, drop by dro
at first, into the butter cream, beating all the time. Plac
one meringue circle on a serving plate, cover with ha
the chocolate cream. Place the second meringue circle o
top, and cover with the rest of the chocolate cream
Finally, place the third meringue circle on top and cove
with grated chocolate.

This is best made the day before it is required and kep
in a cool place.

Menu 4

Avocado Pears

2 avocado pears	6 tbs. olive oil
2 tbs. cider vinegar	salt and pepper

These are best prepared just before eating. Wipe the pears with a damp cloth and cut each in half. Carefully remove and discard the large stone. Mix together the cider vinegar, olive oil and enough salt and pepper to season well. Brush the cut surface of the pears with this dressing and pour some into the cavity left by the stone. Serve the rest of the dressing in a small jug.

Cheese Fritters

This is a good recipe for when the guests are unfamiliar with vegetarian food.

1 pint milk	6 oz. finely grated cheese
1 small whole onion, peeled	1 heaped tbs. chopped parsley
	1 level tsp. mixed seasoning
1 bay leaf	small pinch cayenne, or
1 clove	½ level tsp. dry mustard
4 oz. semolina	

Coating: 1 large beaten egg; toasted crumbs

Put milk, onion, bay leaf and clove in saucepan. Heat until almost boiling. Draw off heat and leave for 10 to 15 mins. Then remove onion, bay leaf and clove. Reboil the milk and sprinkle in semolina, stirring all the time. Simmer until very thick – about 2 mins. Remove from heat and beat in cheese, parsley, seasoning, pepper and mustard. Spread smoothly over a wet plate or board and smooth with a palette knife dipped in water. Leave until quite cold. Cut into 8 pieces, coat with egg, then bread-crumbs, and fry in hot deep or shallow fat until crisp and golden. Drain well. These can be fried beforehand, drained and placed on a baking sheet in a moderate oven to heat through when required.

Coffee Cream Mould

2 eggs
1 oz. cornflour
3 oz. caster sugar
1 level tbs. powdered instant coffee
1 level tbs. drinking chocolate

4 level tsp. agar agar
3 tbs. cold water
¾ pint milk
1 small can evaporated milk

Separate the eggs. Mix the cornflour and sugar, coffee powder, drinking chocolate, agar agar, and cold water with enough of the cold milk to make a smooth paste. Put the remaining milk on to heat. Gradually pour the hot milk on to the mixture, stirring; return to pan. Bring to boil and simmer for 3 mins., stirring continuously. Remove from heat and allow to cool slightly, then stir in evaporated milk. Whisk egg whites until stiff and fold into mixture. Turn into a two-pint mould which has been rinsed in cold water and leave to set.

Chocolate Sauce

4 level tbs. drinking chocolate
¼ pint water

½ oz. butter
2 tbs. milk or cream
whipped cream if desired

Make the chocolate sauce by placing drinking chocolate and water in a saucepan. Bring to boil stirring, and simmer uncovered over a low heat for 10 mins., stirring occasionally. Remove from heat and stir in butter and milk. Allow to cool.

The mould and sauce can be made beforehand and left in a cool place. When ready to serve, dip mould into a bowl of hand-hot water and invert on to serving dish. Pour a little chocolate sauce over mould, and top with whipped cream if desired. Serve rest of chocolate sauce separately.

Menu 5

Oranges

6 large oranges   fresh mint leaves
8 glacé cherries,
  quartered

Peel the oranges and cut into thin rounds, then cut each round into 4 or 8 pieces, depending on size. Divide between 4 glasses and sprinkle with quartered cherries and fresh mint leaves. Leave in a cool place until ready to serve.

Stuffed Peppers

This again is a useful recipe for guests unfamiliar with vegetarian food.

1 medium-sized onion	4 oz. walnuts
1 large clove garlic	1 tsp. lemon juice
1 tsp. basil	salt and pepper, sugar
2 tbs. vegetable or olive oil	4 green peppers cornflakes
2 oz. brown rice	1–2 oz. grated cheese
1 bay leaf	parsley or lemon to garnish
1 can tomato juice	

Peel and chop the onion and garlic and cook with the basil in the oil until soft but not brown – 10 mins. Wash the rice and pick out any brown or hard pieces. Add rice, bay leaf, and half the tomato juice to the onion mixture, and bring to the boil. Then turn down the heat very low and cook for 30 mins. Add walnuts, milled, and lemon juice, and season carefully with salt and pepper, adding a little more tomato juice if necessary, to make a soft consistency.

Wash the peppers and remove the tops. Scoop out all the seeds and rinse the insides of the peppers. Put 2″ water into a pan large enough to take the peppers. Bring water to boil, then add peppers and remove from heat. Leave peppers in the water with the lid on the pan for 5 mins., then drain them and fill with stuffing. Put them on a large ovenproof dish. Add pinch of salt and pinch of sugar to the remaining tomato juice and pour this round the peppers. The peppers can be left prepared for several hours. When ready to cook them, sprinkle the top of each with cornflakes or breadcrumbs and a little grated cheese. Cook in a slow oven, 300° F., gas mark 2, for $\frac{1}{2}$ to $\frac{3}{4}$ hour. Serve garnished with fresh parsley or lemon.

Fruit Shortbreads

4 oz. butter
2 oz. brown sugar
6 oz. plain flour
large can peach slices or
  1 lb. fresh strawberries
  when in season

$\frac{1}{2}$ pint double cream
  (whipped)
chopped toasted almonds
caster sugar

Cream the butter and sugar until light, then beat in the flour. Press the mixture into 2 sandwich tins and bake in slow oven 300° F., gas mark 2, for 30 mins. Cool and remove from tins. These shortbread circles may be made a day or two in advance and stored in an airtight tin. Put one circle on a serving dish and place half the peach slices or hulled strawberries with sugar if required, on top and cover with half of the cream. Place other shortbread circle on top, and the rest of the peach slices or strawberries and sugar, on top of that. Decorate with the rest of the whipped cream and toasted almonds. This can be assembled a few hours beforehand and left in a cool place until required.

Menu 6

Egg and Cucumber Hors D'œuvre

3 eggs, hardboiled	salt and freshly ground black
½ cucumber	pepper
¼ pint plain yoghourt	pinch dill (optional)
2 tbs. chopped chives	4 well-shaped lettuce leaves

Chop the eggs finely. Peel and chop cucumber into ¼″ dice. Combine eggs, cucumber, yoghourt and chives and season with salt and pepper and a pinch of dill if liked. Chill until required, then serve each portion on a lettuce leaf.

Okra Curry with Trimmings

This is another useful recipe when the guests are completely unfamiliar with vegetarian food.

½ lb. leeks	1 heaped tbs. plain flour
1 small cauliflower	1 level tbs. turmeric powder
½ lb. potatoes	2 oz. vegetable fat
2 small onions	1 dessertsp. curry powder
1 small cooking apple	pinch coriander seed
½ lb. tomatoes	3 rounded tbs. mango chutney
1 can Okra (ladies'	½ pint water
fingers)	1 heaped tsp. salt
or celery hearts	¼ tsp. pepper

Wash leeks well, trim and cut into pieces. Wash cauliflower and divide into pieces. Peel and slice the onions and potatoes; peel and chop apple. Wash and chop tomatoes. Mix flour and turmeric in a large bowl. Toss vegetables in this. Melt fat in pan, throw in vegetables and fry lightly, stirring occasionally. Add apple, tomatoes, curry powder, coriander, chutney and water. Season and cook for 30 mins. Drain water from Okra or celery hearts, cut the latter into slices, add to curry and heat through. This dish can be made beforehand and simply warmed up at serving time. The rice (see below) can also be re-heated in a steamer or in a dish over a pan of boiling water.

Brown Rice

Put 8 oz. brown rice in pan with 1 dessertspoonful vegetable oil. Add enough water to *well* cover the rice. Bring to the boil, cover with a tight-fitting lid and simmer gently for 20 mins. Drain if necessary.

Trimmings

Serve curry with any or all of the following trimmings, which can be prepared in advance and left in their serving bowls in a cool place: (1) mango chutney, (2) sliced hardboiled eggs, (3) blanched salted almonds or cashew nuts, (4) sliced skinned tomatoes, (5) sliced bananas tossed in lemon juice, (6) desiccated coconut, (7) onions sliced in rings and covered with a dressing of 6 tablespoonfuls olive oil and 2 tablespoonfuls cider vinegar.

Orange Sorbet

4 oz. caster sugar	juice of $\frac{1}{2}$ lemon
$\frac{1}{2}$ pint water	2 egg whites
4 large oranges	shiny green leaves

Simmer the sugar and water together over a low heat for 10 mins., then cool. Meanwhile, cut the tops off the oranges and using a grapefruit knife, carefully scoop out the flesh keeping the orange skins whole. Set the orange skins on one side. Sieve, or liquidise the orange flesh, add the lemon juice and make up to $\frac{1}{2}$ pint with extra orange juice if necessary, then add to the cooled sugar syrup. Freeze until it begins to set round the edges, then beat thoroughly. Whisk the egg whites until stiff and fold into the orange mixture. Re-freeze until frozen but still soft

Spoon into the orange-skin 'cups', replace lids and serve on a plate surrounded by shiny non-poisonous green leaves – bay leaves are ideal, or a few rose leaves.

Orange sorbet can be prepared beforehand and left in the freezer until required (but do not let it freeze too hard).

Menu 7 (Christmas)

Maraschino Melon

1 small ripe melon   1 jar cocktail cherries

Cut melon in half and remove seeds. Chop melon flesh or use a vegetable scoop. Divide melon and cherries between 4 dishes, and top up with liquid from the cherries.

Mushroom Nutmeat and Stuffing Balls

1 large onion	1 egg
2 oz. margarine	$\frac{1}{2}$ pint milk or milk and water
$\frac{1}{4}$ lb. mushrooms	8 oz. ground cashew nuts
1 tsp. thyme	salt and pepper
2 tbs. ground rice	toasted crumbs

Peel and chop the onion and cook in the margarine with the washed and chopped mushrooms and thyme until soft but not brown, about 10 mins. Add the ground rice, stir well, add the milk and cook until thickened. Beat in egg and cook for 5 mins. Remove from heat and liquidise or pass through a mouli. Stir in the nuts and seasoning. Pile into a bread tin or casserole, which has been greased, and coated with crumbs. Cook in a moderate oven, 350° F., gas mark 4, for 1 hour.

This can be prepared on Christmas Eve and left in a cool place ready for cooking on Christmas Day. Serve with stuffing balls and bread sauce.

Stuffing Balls

8 oz. suenut or vegetable
  cooking fat
1 lb. soft brown breadcrumbs
4 good tbs. chopped parsley
2 tsp. mixed herbs

grated rind of 1 lemon
  and 1 tbs. juice
1 small onion grated
1 egg

Grate suenut or cooking fat and mix all ingredients together. Form into little balls and fry until golden brown; or roast in hot fat in the top of the oven while the nutroast is cooking.

Bread Sauce

1 onion, peeled
3 cloves
½ pint milk
2 oz. fresh white
  breadcrumbs

¼ tsp. nutmeg
½ oz. butter
1 tbs. cream
salt and pepper

Simmer the onion and cloves in the milk over a very gentle heat for 15 mins., then remove onion and stir in all the other ingredients and season to taste.

Christmas Pudding

Make this in advance according to recipe on page 134. As an alternative to the traditional pudding, orange soufflé can be served.

Orange Soufflé

3 small oranges
½ lemon
3 eggs
3 oz. caster sugar
½ oz. agar agar

¼ pint evaporated milk
crystallised violets
whipped cream and
  angelica to decorate

Prepare a straight-sided casserole dish or soufflé dish

by tying a band of greaseproof paper round it extending about 4″ above the rim of the dish.

Strain the orange and lemon juice into a china bowl and stir in the egg yolks and sugar. Whisk this mixture over a pan of boiling water until it is thick (like double cream) and creamy. Then gradually stir in the agar agar, dissolved in a little water. Whisking well between each addition. Allow the mixture to cool slightly.

Meanwhile, whip the evaporated milk until really thick, and fold into the orange mixture. Beat the egg whites until stiff and standing in peaks, and fold them in gently. Pour the mixture into the soufflé dish, letting it overflow the rim of the dish into the greaseproof band. Leave in a cool place until set. Carefully remove paper, and decorate the top and sides of the soufflé with whirls of whipped cream, crystallised violets and angelica leaves.

VII

THE USE OF
WHOLEMEAL FLOUR

100% wholemeal flour is used in the vegetarian diet, for it contains the whole of the wheat and is therefore properly balanced and a valuable source of nutrition, containing protein, minerals and roughage. This flour is obtainable from Health Food Stores and many grocers and bakers. The 100% stone-ground variety of wholemeal flour is made by various firms, including Allinsons and Prewetts, and there are various types, such as plain, self-raising and cake-flour. We prefer to use plain for all purposes, and add baking powder when needed.

Because of the different constitution of white and wholemeal flour some people find that they have difficulty at first in using the wholemeal variety, especially for pastry. Brown flour is not as starchy or glutinous, and one soon gets used to it, and it is possible to make deliciously light cakes, pastry, puddings and biscuits with it Because of its different texture, a little more baking powder is required, so in adapting white flour recipes it is best to use rounded teaspoons of baking powder, instead of level ones. In recipes needing a lot of raising agent, such as scones, use the amount stated plus a beaten egg. An extra egg in cake recipes will give a lighter result, and of course renders the mixture more nourishing.

All the recipes in this section are quick to make. In each case 'plain flour' means plain (no raising agent contained) 100% wholewheat stone-ground.

How to Make Wholemeal Pastry

8 oz. plain flour
4 oz. vegetable shortening, or vegetable
   shortening and margarine mixed
2 level tsp. baking powder
pinch salt
approx. 2 tbs. cold water

1. Sift together the salt, baking powder and flour.

2. Rub in the fat with the finger tips until the mixture resembles fine breadcrumbs, then add the cold water quickly, mixing lightly.

3. Gather the mixture up into a ball and place it on a large sheet of greaseproof paper. Put another sheet of greaseproof paper on top and roll the pastry through this to the required size.

4. If you require to line a flan tin, or cover a pie with the pastry, all you have to do is to peel off the top layer of paper, lift the pastry on the bottom paper, poise it over the tin or pie, turn it over, press it down, then when it is neatly in place gently peel off the greaseproof paper, pressing the pastry down as you do so. This simple, clean method eliminates all those juggling tricks with pastry round the rolling-pin, and the horrible mess of flour on the pastry board. It is also the answer for those who say that they can never make wholemeal pastry hold together, because even the most fragile variety will hold together when transferred to the pie from the greaseproof paper. Bake in a hot oven 450° F., gas mark 8.

This pastry can be used to replace white pastry in all recipes. If 'baking blind' do not bother to fill the flan with beans, etc. Just prick the bottom of the flan lightly and this will be quite adequate to stop the pastry rising.

Pastry-making is still further simplified if you rub fat into at least 1½ lb. flour at a time, and store the rubbed-in mixture in a jar in a cool place or fridge. It will keep for at least a fortnight.

This rubbed-in mixture can be used to make a quick crumble topping for fruit by adding a little brown sugar. It can also form the basis of a quick fruit cake:

Five-Minute Fruit Cake

12 oz. rubbed-in mixture	8 oz.–1 lb. cleaned
4 oz. brown (barbados) sugar	mixed dried fruit
(obtainable Health Food	2 eggs
Stores)	milk

Put the rubbed-in mixture into a large bowl and stir in the sugar and fruit. Beat the eggs lightly. Add to the mixture with enough milk to make a soft dropping consistency and stir thoroughly together. Place mixture in a 6″ or 7″ cake tin lined with greaseproof paper. Bake in pre-heated moderate oven, 350° F., gas mark 4, for $1\frac{1}{4}$ to $1\frac{1}{2}$ hours.

Dundee Cake

10 oz. plain flour	6 oz. currants
1 heaped tsp. baking	2 oz. candied peel
powder	2 oz. glacé cherriës, halved
6 oz. butter	1 tsp. grated lemon rind
6 oz. barbados sugar	2 oz. ground almonds
3 eggs	1 oz. blanched split almonds
8 oz. sultanas	milk

Sift the flour with the baking powder and mix in the bran which is left in the sieve. Cream the butter and sugar until light and fluffy, then add the beaten eggs, one at a time, slowly, beating all the time, adding a little flour if the mixture starts to curdle. (It curdles because the egg is being added too quickly.) Fold in the flour and all the other ingredients, adding a little milk if necessary but do not make the mixture too soft. Put into a 7″ tin which has been lined with 2 layers of greased greaseproof paper, and arrange the split almonds on top. Bake in a moderate oven, 350° F., gas mark 4, for about 2 hours, or until a warmed knife inserted into it comes out clean.

Wholemeal Christmas Cake

1½ oz. whole almonds	6 oz. sultanas, cleaned
6 oz. plain flour	6 oz. raisins, cleaned
1 level tsp. mixed spice	3 oz. ground almonds
6 oz. butter	2 oz. glacé pineapple fairly
6 oz. soft brown sugar	finely chopped
5 eggs	1 oz. angelica fairly finely
1 tbs. treacle	chopped
9 oz. currants, cleaned	4 oz. glacé cherries
3 oz. chopped mixed peel	1 tbs. brandy (optional)
grated rind and juice of 1	
lemon	

Place almonds in a small pan. Cover with cold water. Bring to the boil. Drain, and remove skins. Chop almonds roughly.

Turn on the oven and set at slow (300° F., gas mark 2). Grease an 8″ round tin, line with 3 thicknesses of greased greaseproof paper. Tie brown paper around the outside of tin so that it extends 2″ above the top; secure with string.

Sift together the flour and mixed spice into a basin, mixing in the bran left in the sieve. Cream the butter and brown sugar in a bowl until light and fluffy. Add the eggs, one by one, beating well after each. Add a little flour if mixture curdles. Stir in treacle. Fold in flour. Stir in currants, peel, rind, juice of lemon, sultanas, raisins, ground almonds, glacé pineapple and angelica.

Wash the glacé cherries under hot running water and cut into halves. Add to bowl and mix well. Put mixture into prepared tin. Bake in the centre of the pre-heated oven for $4\frac{1}{2}$ to 5 hours or until a warmed knife inserted into it comes out clean (as above). Should cake need further cooking, replace in oven, but watch carefully.

Turn out cake carefully on to a wire rack to cool. When it is quite cold, remove paper.

If you are using brandy, prick the top of cold cake with a knife. Pour the brandy over the top and allow to soak in. Wrap the cake in two layers of greaseproof paper and store in an airtight tin until ready for icing.

Quick Sponge Cake

3 oz. plain flour	$\frac{1}{2}$ tsp. vanilla essence
1 tsp. baking powder	1 oz. butter
3 eggs	2 tbs. milk
3 oz. caster (or barbados) sugar	

Sieve together the flour and baking powder. Separate the eggs. Beat the whites to a stiff froth, then lightly beat in the yolks. Add the sugar, and fold in the flour and baking powder. Heat the butter and milk in a pan until the butter has melted. Add to the egg mixture and flavour with vanilla essence. Grease two 7″ sandwich tins, divide the mixture between them, and bake at 350° F., gas mark 4, for 20 mins. When cold, remove from tins and sandwich with warm jam, or cream or butter icing, and dredge with caster sugar. This is a small, very light cake which is best eaten within two or three days (and invariably is!)

Victoria Sandwich

4 oz. butter or margarine	3 eggs
4 oz. barbados or caster sugar	4 oz. plain flour
	1 level tsp. baking powder

Cream butter or margarine with sugar till light and fluffy. Add beaten eggs very gradually, adding a little flour if necessary to prevent curdling. Sift together flour and baking powder, mixing in the bran left in the sieve, and fold in gently. Put into two 7" greased tins and bake in a moderate oven, 375° F., gas mark 5, for 20 mins. Fill with jam, cream or butter icing.

Gingerbread

2 oz. golden syrup	3 oz. barbados sugar
6 oz. black treacle	2 eggs
4 oz. margarine	2 oz. chopped walnuts, candied
8 oz. plain flour	peel or crystallised ginger
2 level tsp. baking	(optional)
powder	$\frac{1}{2}$ tsp. bicarbonate of soda
$\frac{1}{2}$ tsp. ground ginger	1 cup milk

Grease a square tin and line with layers of greased greaseproof paper. Melt and blend the syrup, treacle and margarine in a pan over a moderate heat. Sieve flour with spices and baking powder, add sugar, and nuts or peel. Make a well in centre and pour in warmed treacle mixture and the beaten eggs. Quickly beat in the milk with the bicarbonate of soda dissolved in it, and pour mixture into tin. Cook in a moderate oven, 350° F., gas mark 4 for $1\frac{1}{4}$ hours or until well risen and firm to touch.

Rock Cakes

12 oz. rubbed-in mixture or
   8 oz. plain flour
   4 oz. fat   }rubbed together
   1 heaped tsp. baking powder
4 oz. barbados sugar
1 level tsp. mixed spice
4 oz. mixed dried fruit
1 egg
granulated sugar

Mix the sugar and spice into the rubbed-in mixture add the fruits and beaten egg and mix well. One egg should be sufficient to make the right consistency which should be 'crumbly' and the mixture should only just hold together; only if necessary a *very* little milk can be added. Put rough piles of the mixture on to a greased baking sheet. Sprinkle with granulated sugar and bake in a hot oven, 450° F., gas mark 8, for 12 to 15 mins. (Makes approx. 12.)

Date Slice

If you make a little extra pastry when making a pie or flan, these nutritious biscuits are quickly made and are popular with the family.

> 6 oz. shortcrust pastry
> 8 oz stoned cooking dates
> juice of 1 lemon or 1 orange

Line a 7″ sandwich tin with half the pastry. Heat the dates and lemon or orange juice in a pan until the dates are soft. Beat with a wooden spoon until smooth. Put this date mixture on the pastry-lined tin, cover with the rest of the pastry, prick the top, and bake in a hot oven 450° F., gas mark 8, for about 10 mins. Dredge with caster sugar, and serve cut in slices.

Shortbread

> 8 oz. butter or margarine
> 4 oz. brown sugar
> 12 oz. plain flour

Beat butter or margarine until creamy, beat in sugar and mix until well blended, then gradually beat in flour. Press into a swiss roll tin and bake in a slow oven 300° F., gas mark 2, for 30 mins, until golden and crisp. Mark into slices while still hot, allow to cool in tin, then remove and dredge with caster sugar.

Rich Vanilla Biscuits

2 oz. margarine or butter	4 oz. plain flour
1 oz. cooking fat	1 level tsp. baking powder
1½ oz. sugar	1 tsp. vanilla essence

Cream margarine, fat and sugar. Sieve together the flour and baking powder and stir into the creamed mixture. Add the vanilla essence. Knead lightly, roll into smooth balls. Put on an ungreased tin and bake for 20 mins. in centre of a moderate oven, 375° F., gas mark 5.

Chocolate Krakolets

1 bar plain raw sugar chocolate
enough wholemeal flakes or cornflakes to make a firm mixture

Break the chocolate into pieces and melt by standing it in a bowl in the top of a steamer or in a pan of hot water, or use a double saucepan. Stir in enough wholemeal flakes or cornflakes to become coated with the chocolate. Put a tablespoonful into paper cases and allow to get cold before serving.

Cheese Biscuits

8 oz. butter or margarine	12 oz. plain flour
4 oz. cheddar cheese, grated	pinch cayenne pepper

Rub fat in flour, then blend in the cheese, kneading until all the ingredients are mixed and hold together. Press into a swiss roll tin. Bake at 300° F., gas mark 2, for 30 mins. Mark into sections while hot, allow to cool, then remove from tin.

Christmas Pudding

8 oz. currants	1½ tsp. mixed spice
4 oz. sultanas	8 oz. barbados sugar
4 oz. raisins	4 oz. soft brown breadcrumbs
4 oz. candied peel	8 oz. vegetable suenut, shredded
1 oz. blanched almonds	
4 oz. plain flour	rind and juice of 1 lemon
½ tsp. salt	2 eggs
½ tsp. nutmeg (grated)	1 tbs. treacle
½ tsp. ground ginger	approx. 4 tbs. milk or milk and rum

Wash and dry fruit; stone and chop raisins, finely chop peel and blanched almonds. Sieve flour with salt and spices. Mix all dry ingredients, add fruits, nuts and peel, lemon rind and strained juice. Beat eggs and stir into mixture, then mix in treacle. Add sufficient milk and rum mixture, or plain milk, to make a soft mixture which will fall heavily from the spoon when shaken. Stir all well together. Put mixture into well-greased 2-pint basin, or two 1-pint basins, and fill to 1″ from top. Cover with greased greaseproof paper and tie on a pudding cloth, or cover with greased tinfoil. Steam for 4 hours. Store in a dry place; steam for another 3 hours before serving. This pudding serves 8 people.

Mincemeat

1 lb. currants	1 lb. shredded vegetable suenut
1 lb. sultanas	
1 lb. raisins	¾ lb. barbados sugar
1 lb. cooking apples	½ tsp. salt
2 oz. glacé cherries	½ tsp. nutmeg (grated)
2 oz. dates	½ tsp. ground ginger
2 oz. blanched almonds	1 tsp. mixed spice
6 oz. candied peel	2 lemons
	2 tangerines
	¼ pint rum or brandy

Clean and dry fruit. Stone and chop raisins. Peel, core and chop or mince apples finely. Chop peel, cherries, dates and blanched almonds. Mix all together in a large basin with shredded suenut. Stir in sugar, spices and salt. Grate in rind of 1 lemon and 1 tangerine, and add juice of 2 lemons and 2 tangerines. Add spirit. Mix thoroughly with wooden spoon. Put into clean jars and store in a cool, dry place. This makes 7 lbs. mincemeat.

At Christmastime use wholemeal pastry to line tartlet tins for individual mincepies, or make one large pie by lining a pie dish or sandwich tin with pastry, filling with mincemeat and topping with more pastry. When cooked dredge with caster sugar.

Scones

1 dessertsp. fine oatmeal (Prewetts)	pinch salt
	1 oz. margarine or fat
4 oz. plain flour	1 oz. sultanas
1 heaped tsp. baking powder	6 tbs. milk
1 oz. brown sugar	

Sift together oatmeal, flour and baking powder and pinch salt and sugar. Rub in fat until mixture resembles breadcrumbs, mix to a soft pliable consistency with milk. Press out on to a floured board to $\frac{1}{2}''$ thickness and cut with a 1″ cutter. Or shape into rounds on a floured baking tin and cut across and across into 8 sections. Bake at 350° F., gas mark 4, for 15 mins.

Variation: use 1 tablespoonful black treacle and only 4 tablespoonfuls milk, blending the two together before adding.

Ten-Minute Bread

2 lbs. plain flour	1 oz. dried yeast
1–2 oz. fresh yeast (can be ordered from a baker) or	1 tbs. barbados sugar
	2 tsp. salt
	$1\frac{1}{2}$ pints warm water

Put the yeast and sugar into a large mixing bowl with ½ pint lukewarm water and leave them for 5 mins. (or 10 mins. if using dried yeast) or until yeast 'breaks'. Meanwhile weigh out the flour and grease two 2–lb. loaf tins, and turn the oven to 250° F., gas mark ½. Then tip the flour into the yeast mixture, add the salt and the rest of the water (1 pint). Mix well to a fairly sloppy consistency using scrubbed hands, and pile into the tins. Place in the oven (or in a warm place) until the dough reaches the tops of the tins (takes anything from 10 to 30 mins.). Turn up the oven to 425° F., gas mark 7, and leave for 40 mins. Remove from tins when slightly cooled, and leave to cool on a wire rack.

Crusty Round Loaves

These take longer to make than the ten-minute loaf, but are a pleasant change.

2 oz. fresh, or 1 oz. dried yeast	1 pint warm water
1 tbs. brown sugar	2 lbs. plain flour
	2 tsp. salt

Put the yeast, sugar and ¼ pint of the water into a large bowl and leave until dissolved and slightly frothy. Mix in half the flour, the salt and the rest of the water (¾ pint), stir well and tip the rest of the flour on top but do not mix in. Leave in a warm place for 45 to 60 mins. until the mixture has risen and doubled in bulk. Mix in the loose flour and knead for 5 mins. Shape into two round loaves and place on a greased baking sheet. Cover with a wet cloth. Leave in a warm place for 20 to 30 mins. until they have risen about half as big again. (If you turn on the oven at this stage, the loaves can be left in the grill compartment on a folded towel getting the heat from the oven as it warms up.) Prick the tops, bake in a hot oven, 450° F., gas mark 8, for about 25 mins., until golden and crisp. Cool on a wire rack.

Quick Baking Powder Loaf

½ lb. plain flour   ¼ pint plus 2 tbs. milk
4 level tsp. baking powder

Sift the flour and baking powder together into a large bowl. Mix quickly to a soft dough with the milk. Turn on to a floured board and knead lightly for a minute or two till the dough is smooth. Shape into a round with your hands and place on a floured baking sheet. Brush the top with milk to give a nice golden brown crust and bake in the centre of a hot oven, 425° F., gas mark 7, for 25 to 30 mins.

This is a quickly made 'emergency' loaf, and quite delicious eaten warm with plenty of butter.

Rolls

1 oz. fresh or ½ oz. dried   ½ pint warm water
   yeast   1 lb. plain flour
1 tsp. brown sugar   1 tsp. salt

Put the yeast, sugar and ¼ pint of the water into a large bowl and leave until dissolved and slightly frothy. Mix in half the flour, the salt and the rest of the water (¼ pint), stir well and tip the rest of the flour on top but do not mix. Leave in a warm place for 45 to 60 mins. until the mixture has risen and doubled in bulk. Mix in the loose flour and knead for five minutes. Shape into rolls, half the size required for the finished rolls, and place well apart on a greased baking sheet. Cover with a wet cloth and leave in a warm place for 20 to 30 mins. until they have risen. (If you turn on the oven at this stage, they can be left in the grill compartment on a folded towel, getting the heat from the oven as it warms up.) Prick the tops, and bake in a hot oven, 450° F., gas mark 8, for about 10 mins., until golden and crisp. Place on a wire rack and cool.

VIII

PARTIES

The vegetarian diet lends itself delightfully to party fare and there is no need at all for the hostess to feel compelled to resort to salmon, chicken, sausages, or paté or any other flesh foods in order to provide a varied and attractive spread.

Here are a few well-tried ideas and suggestions which have proved popular in the past and can be varied and adapted to suit individual needs. For a winter buffet party we usually like to start with a hot soup, served with warm, crisp, brown rolls, french bread, croûtons, and perhaps grated cheese.

This is followed by a selection of any of the following savouries, which can be prepared beforehand and arranged attractively on a large table with a good supply of paper napkins as well as plates and cutlery, ready for people to serve themselves.

1. SAVOURY BOATS OR TARTLETS

Make wholemeal tartlets and bake blind, or put wholemeal pastry round boat moulds and bake. When cold, fill with a thick creamy white sauce flavoured with any of the following:

Chopped asparagus tips, mayonnaise and parsley

Fried mushrooms and yeast extract

Hardboiled eggs and cheese

Grated cheese seasoned with salt and cayenne pepper, and chopped chives

Grated nuts with salt and pepper, yeast extract and grated onion.

2. CREAM CHEESE TITBITS

Pipe or spoon cream cheese on to any of the following bases. Garnish with a sprinkling of paprika pepper, olives, pieces of gherkin, grape, parsley, chopped chives, chopped nuts or sultanas.

Sliced cucumber
Sticks of celery cut into 3″ lengths
Pieces of pepper, canned or fresh, de-seeded
Pineapple cubes
Halved tomatoes with seeds removed
Small crisp lettuce leaves.

3. TARTEX TITBITS

Spread or pipe Tartex or other savoury spread on to any of the following bases. Garnish with parsley, lemon 'butterflies', or tomato slices.

Crisp fried bread
Wholemeal toast pieces
Tiny scones
Small cheese biscuits.

4. PEANUT BALLS

8 oz. cream cheese   4 oz. salted peanuts

Place the peanuts between two sheets of greaseproof paper and crush them with a rolling pin. Break the cream cheese into little pieces about the size of a hazel nut and roll each one in the peanut crumbs until well coated.

5. CRISP SAUSALATAS

Wash the jelly off canned sausages, roll them in toasted crumbs and bake in oil or fat at 450° F., gas mark 8, for $\frac{3}{4}$ hour, turning them occasionally to make sure they are evenly browned. Drain well on kitchen paper. Cut each in half and spike each half on to a cocktail stick. Serve cold on a large dish or spiked into a grapefruit or cabbage to form a hedgehog.

6. DEVILLED EGGS

6 hardboiled eggs	¼ tsp. made mustard
3 oz. cream cheese	½ small onion chopped finely
4 level tbs. mayonnaise	⅓ tsp. curry powder
salt and pepper	

Slice the shelled eggs in half lengthwise. Remove yolks carefully with a teaspoon and set aside whites. Mash the yolks with a fork, blending in the cream cheese, mayonnaise, salt and pepper, mustard, onion and curry powder.

Fill the egg whites with heaped teaspoonfuls of the mixture, or use a star nozzle on a large piping bag if preferred. Garnish with parsley or a sprinkling of paprika pepper.

7. STUFFED DATES

Remove the stones from dessert dates, and stuff them with a nut kernel or cream cheese.

8. NUT SAVOURY SLICES

Cold mushroom nutmeat (see page 123) or stuffed nutmeat (see page 111) may be sliced thinly, cut into fingers and served on a large plate with watercress and parsley to garnish.

9. ALMOND SQUARES

Make an almond nutmeat mixture (see page 63), press into a swiss roll tin so that it is about ½" deep. Bake at 350° F., gas mark 4, for 30 mins. until brown and crisp. Cut into 1" squares, and serve cold with a piece of pickle speared on to each with a cocktail stick.

10. PARTY LOAF

1 small wholemeal loaf	¼ lb. salted peanuts
½ lb. cream cheese	(crushed between sheets
¼ lb. butter	of greaseproof paper with
	a rolling pin)

Fillings (other variations can be used)

2 large cans Tartex	1 tbs. chopped chives
2 oz. butter	1 tsp. yeast extract
2 tbs. chopped parsley	

Slice crusts off loaf and also the rounded top to make a square loaf. Cut the loaf lengthwise into four slices. Butter both sides of all the slices except top and bottom ones, which should be buttered on one side only. Sandwich the slices together with the following fillings and press down firmly.

1st layer: Tartex
2nd layer: Butter beaten with chopped parsley, chives and yeast extract
3rd layer: Tartex

Coat the assembled loaf on sides and top with cream cheese. Roll the sides in peanuts and garnish the top with parsley, chives, tomatoes, olives or gherkins. Serve whole or already sliced.

11. CHEESE BISCUITS (RICH)

4 oz. butter	4 oz. grated cheese
5 oz. plain flour	cayenne pepper
2 egg yolks	salt

Rub butter into flour, add egg yolks, cheese, cayenne and salt. Press into swiss roll tin and bake in a slow oven, 325° F., gas mark 3, for 20 mins. Mark into thin fingers and allow to cool before removing from tin.

12. HEDGEHOGS

Spear any of the following on to cocktail sticks and stick into a large grapefruit or cabbage cut so that it stands level.

Olives	Pineapple cubes
Gherkins	Pickled walnuts
Pearl onions	Stoned dates

13. SALTED NUTS

Fry blanched almonds or cashew nuts in hot oil over a moderate heat until golden brown, turning frequently to prevent burning. Drain on kitchen paper and sprinkle with salt, and cayenne pepper if liked.

14. PARSLEY ROLLS

1 small wholemeal loaf	2 heaped tbs. chopped parsley
½ lb. butter	squeeze of lemon juice

Cut all the crusts off the small loaf and slice fairly thinly lengthwise. Beat the butter until light and creamy, and add the parsley and lemon juice. Spread the parsley butter thickly on the pieces of bread, roll them up tightly like a swiss roll and slice each one into rounds about ¼″ thick.

15. SALAD

Serve bite-sized pieces of crisp lettuce, cucumber, cress, watercress or radishes, in a salad bowl.

16. SWEET

We usually end the meal with a simple, light sweet: fruit salad with cream or ice-cream; fresh peach halves brushed with lemon juice, topped with cream and garnished with whole blanched almonds; fruit jelly; fruit syllabub – equal parts of fruit purée and whipped cream or whipped evaporated milk served with sponge finger biscuits; or unadorned fresh fruit.

For a Christmas party – mince pies and cream.

IX

FEEDING BABIES AND INVALIDS

The diets of babies and invalids are similar in that small quantities are taken, and their food needs to be finer and more easily digestible than ordinary meals.

BABIES

CEREALS

The first solid food that a baby has is usually a little cereal with milk, either before or after his milk feed. Personally, I think it is best not to try to introduce this extra food until the baby is obviously not satisfied with milk alone, usually at about $2\frac{1}{2}$ to 3 months. Many of the baby cereals on the market have extra protein in the form of bone meal added to them, and so are obviously unsuitable for vegetarian babies. There are, however, wholewheat cereals obtainable from Health Food Stores, and we have found these very satisfactory. We have found packet muesli (the Swiss brand) ground very finely in a coffee mill and mixed with boiled milk, even better. Babies seem to love it, and it is very nutritious. Frugrains are also very popular with young babies. Use the small powdery Frugrains, and pour milk over. If this is left for a few minutes the Frugrains become softened and are suitable for quite young babies.

ADDITIONS TO VEGETABLE PURÉES

Protein can be added to the canned sieved baby foods, or to home-made purées in the form of:

Finely grated cheese
Very finely grated nuts
Nut butters or creams
Skimmed milk powder
Egg yolk or whole coddled egg, mashed
Cooked lentils

A thick lentil soup (see page 29), flavoured with Marmite, and made with extra milk, is a nourishing and popular savoury, as are creamed mashed potatoes with cheese.

When the baby gets used to these foods they can gradually become less smooth in texture, preparing him for adult foods.

FRESH FRUIT AND VEGETABLES

From five to six months a baby can chew a piece of raw carrot or apple instead of a rusk, but he will not be able really to eat it at this early age, and so will need to obtain the vitamins present in fruits and vegetables in the form of drinks. Ribena or rose-hip syrup can be diluted and given from one month, and if an electric juice extractor is available *small* quantities of carrot or sweetened apple juice can be given from about three months. Finely grated or chopped raw vegetables can be introduced, mixed in with the sieved vegetables, as soon as the baby is taking the latter well.

RUSKS

From about five months a baby finds great comfort in something hard to bite on. As mentioned above, hard apple or carrot can be given; but make sure that the piece is large enough not to be swallowed accidentally. Rusks can also be made by breaking wholemeal bread into rough pieces and baking in a slow oven until crisp. Vitawheat also makes good rusks, and so do Healthy Life biscuits.

VITAMIN D

Usually this is given in the form of cod liver oil, but this is unsuitable for vegetarian babies, and there is an excellent alternative called Radiostol (*not* Radiostoleum, which contains animal matter). Radiostol is obtainable (on order) from chemists, and a drop added to the breakfast cereal each day ensures an adequate supply of Vitamin D.

Finally, when feeding babies and children it is always helpful psychologically to give small, dainty portions, and to garnish them attractively.

INVALIDS AND OLD PEOPLE

These remarks are general, and do not of course replace the doctor's advice and the needs of specific illnesses where special diets are required. People still sometimes think of a vegetarian diet in terms of large salads and indigestible nut savouries. Therefore we think it is often as well to point out to the doctor how the vegetarian diet can be adapted to the needs of sick people.

In cooking for invalids the main consideration is to get as much nourishment as possible into the small amount of food which they can manage.

SOUPS

Soups are very useful, as these can be fortified and nourishment added in the form of:

Dried milk powder
Grated cheese
Beaten egg
Nut butters and creams
Dried yeast powder

VEGETABLE PURÉES

Baby purées are useful, and additional protein can be stirred into them as suggested for babies.

FRESH FRUIT AND VEGETABLES

The same applies as for the feeding of babies. The juices can be served slightly warmed if desired, but do not overheat or the vital vitamins will be destroyed.

NUTMEATS

Canned nutmeats are useful, being of a very fine texture, and it is also possible to make a very finely textured nutmeat by grating instead of chopping the onions, and using a coffee grinder to grind the nuts really fine.

CHEESE AND EGG SAVOURIES

These are often very suitable for invalids, and the following recipes are particularly good:

Baked cheese soufflé pudding (page 75)
Egg and bread fritters (page 32)
Cheese egg pie (page 67)
Cheese soufflé (page 31)
Jacket potato boats (page 73)

Also the following nut savouries:

Hazel nut pie (page 60)
Hazelnut Mould (page 24)
White nutmeat (page 63)
(if the nuts are very finely grated, as in a
coffee grinder)

MILK PUDDINGS

Another way of introducing protein into the diet is through milky puddings such as ground rice, milk jellies and moulds, rice pudding and egg custards. The milk can be fortified by beating in some dried milk such as Marvel to give extra protein.

Always remember to serve small portions on an attractive tray with pretty and tempting garnishes.

These are some of our favourite invalid dishes:

Semolina Cheese

1 pint milk	4 oz. finely grated cheese
2 oz. semolina	salt and pepper
1 egg, separated	

Season the milk and bring it to the boil, then sprinkle on the semolina, stirring all the time. Continue stirring until thickened. Cook for 5 mins., then remove from the heat, and beat in the egg yolk and cheese. Beat the egg white until stiff and fold in. Serve immediately.

Baked Eggs

4 oz. mushrooms or tomatoes	a little butter
	4 tbs. cream or milk
4 eggs	

Chop the mushrooms or tomatoes and fry lightly in the butter. Put a little of this mixture in the bottom of four ramekin dishes, then add an egg, and lastly 1 tablespoon-ful of cream or milk to each. Sprinkle the tops with salt and a grating of black pepper, place the dishes in a tin containing some boiling water, cover, and simmer gently for 20 to 30 mins., until the eggs are set. Serve at once, with lettuce or endive (when in season), tomatoes, cucumber and chicory boats.

Omelettes

1–2 eggs per person
seasoning to taste
1 oz. butter

When cooking for a number of people it is easier to make several omelettes rather than one large one. Beat the eggs, season with salt and pepper. Heat the omelette pan and melt the butter in it, but do not let it brown. When it bubbles and sizzles pour in the egg mixture, and stir it to spread it evenly over the pan. As the eggs start to set, push back the edges with a palette knife so that the uncooked mixture can run under. Repeat until all the mixture has set. Shake the pan to ensure the omelette has not stuck to the bottom, then slide it down towards the far side of the pan, fold the far edge of the omelette towards the centre, and the other edge over that, and tip it out on to a warm plate. Garnish with parsley and serve immediately with green salad, tomato salad, and perhaps potato salad if a more substantial meal is required.

Fillings

The omelette may be filled with any of the following which should be prepared before the omelette is made, and kept hot, if necessary, until required: grated cheese; cooked sieved spinach; chopped fried mushrooms; chopped fried red pepper; freshly chopped herbs – parsley, tarragon, chives, chervil as obtainable.

Savoury Cheese Custard

3 eggs	4 oz. grated cheese
1 pint milk	salt and pepper
	pinch mustard (optional)

Beat together the eggs and milk and strain into an ovenproof dish. Add the cheese, salt and pepper, and mustard if used. Put the dish into a baking tin with ½″ cold water in it, and bake in a moderate oven, 325° F., gas mark 3, until set. This can be served hot or cold, and may also be cooked in well-greased individual moulds (in which case the cooking time can be reduced) and turned out when cold and served with salad.

Carrageen Mould

½ cup carrageen moss
  or 1 tsp. Gelozone
1 pint milk

pared rind 1 orange or lemon
  (optional)
2 oz. sugar or honey to taste
grated nutmeg

Rinse the carrageen moss thoroughly in warm water and put into a pan with the milk and sugar; or, if using Gelozone, put this into a pan with the milk and sugar, stirring until blended. Add rind if using. Heat milk to boiling, then simmer *very gently* for 10 mins. Strain into a glass dish, grate nutmeg over the top, and leave to set. Serve with stewed fruit if liked.

Egg Custard

3 eggs
1 pint milk or fortified
  milk

2 oz. barbados sugar
½ tsp. vanilla essence
½ tsp. almond essence

Beat the eggs into the warmed milk, add sugar and essences, and strain into an ovenproof dish. Put the dish in a baking tin containing ½" cold water, and bake in a moderate oven, 325° F., gas mark 3, until set. Serve hot or cold.

Egg Whip

This is made in the liquidiser, and is a delicious meal in itself. The ingredients given are for one person.

1 egg
½ pint water

1 orange peeled
2 tbs. honey

Break the egg into the liquidiser and add all the other ingredients. Liquidise until all ingredients are blended, then strain into a glass and serve.

Fortified Milk

1 glass milk   2 tbs. dried skim milk powder

Beat together and serve hot or cold. Especially nourishing for invalids.

X

SLIMMING

It seems a little cynical to end a cookery book with a chapter on slimming, and indeed, if the principles laid out in this book are followed exactly there should be no need for such a chapter. However, it is not always as simple as this; with the pressures of modern life and the availability of quick, fattening snacks, it is all too easy to put on excess weight, jeopardising health and vitality.

If this is your problem, perhaps these suggestions from our own experience will help you to reduce to your correct weight.

The cause of overweight is usually the result of faulty diet over a period, so the first thing to do is to analyse your diet, writing down all you normally eat during the day including snacks, sweets and coffee. Perhaps the diet contains too many of the following foods:

Bread and Biscuits (sweet and savoury)
Cakes and Pastries
Puddings
Rice
Cornflour (including thickened soups, sauces and gravies)
Macaroni
Potatoes
Fruit canned in syrup
Sugar (including that taken in tea and coffee)
Alcohol and fruit squashes
Jam, marmalade, honey and treacle
Ice-cream, blancmange
Sweets and chocolate

Having decided where it is that the diet is fattening, the second thing is to find out the reason for eating the fattening foods. Is it:

(a) Habit formed over a long period and now accepted, e.g. sugar in tea and coffee; biscuits between meals?

(b) Lack of organisation; for instance, not having a proper breakfast or main meal, thus feeling the need for a snack in between?

(c) Emotional stress or nervous tension? Perhaps you seek the comfort of food because of some emotional stress or tension in your life which is making you over-eat. Often people who are plump feel miserable about it and so seek the comfort of sugary and starchy foods and create a vicious circle.

Having decided the root cause of the problem, the next step is to set about curing it.

1. Break all old habits by starting with one or preferably two days on liquids, or liquids and fruits (no bananas). Use a liquidiser or juice extractor if available to make fresh vegetable juice, or use the canned *unsweetened* type. Choose days when you can take life quietly for this cleansing period.

2. If you are really overweight, or if old eating habits are your problem, it may be best to follow this with perhaps a fortnight or so on a quick reducing diet (seek your doctor's advice about this). Such diets are often published in magazines, and meat protein can safely be replaced by the equivalent in cheese or nuts (not cashews). When following savoury recipes substitute cooked celery, onions, leeks or raw grated carrot or 'Cambridge Formula' loaf for breadcrumbs, rice, macaroni, oats or other starchy foods. Use egg to thicken sauces (see recipe at the end of this chapter) and avoid sugar and flour as much as possible. A non-fattening sweetener can be used for a

time, but it is really best not to make a habit of this, but rather to get used to having things less sweet.

3. Once you have lost a little weight you can start on a normal diet, but avoid too much starch. If you want to continue losing weight, try cutting out all sugar every day, and one day cutting out potatoes, the next day cutting out all bread, and if necessary substitute wholemeal starch reduced rolls or Cambridge formula bread. In any case, avoid cakes, biscuits and puddings, and if using canned fruits, try to obtain those which have been canned in water (available from chemists). It is easy to cook family meals and eat the same as the rest of the family, merely giving oneself a smaller portion without pastry or potatoes, and substituting natural yoghourt or fresh fruit for sweet puddings. It is also helpful to start the meal with a clear (unthickened) soup, or fresh unsweetened fruit juice, or grapefruit, as this takes the edge off the appetite.

4. Once you have found your perfect weight, keep it by carefully planning your day's intake of starch. Try to limit the day's starch to two slices of bread and one medium potato, or the equivalent. This can be varied – for instance, you could have a portion of cereal and a slice of toast for breakfast; no starch at lunch, and a potato in the evening. Or you could have a fruit and nut breakfast, a slice of bread for lunch, and a potato and small portion of pastry for the evening meal. Or you could avoid starch all day and have a potato, and a savoury containing rice or breadcrumbs, and some pie for pudding in the evening. In fact, you can choose three average portions from the following during the day and have them as and when you like:

Medium potato
Slice of bread, toast or crispbread
Dish with rice or breadcrumbs, or macaroni or flour
Pastry dish

Breakfast cereal
Sweet pudding

But try to avoid sweets and biscuits for a time; you will then gradually lose the taste for them. Eating in between meals should be avoided; try drinking a glass of water or fresh fruit juice instead, and turning your mind on to some positive activity.

If emotional stress or nervous tension is the root cause of overweight, you may find it better to have frequent small meals rather than three main meals a day. Try taking light main meals, or having one of the following snacks in between instead: an egg beaten up in milk, some yoghourt, some fruit juice with dried yeast stirred into it, or a glass of milk with two tablespoonfuls of skimmed milk powder beaten into it.

If you start to put on weight again, tackle it before it is too late. Have two days on fruit juice or salad (see recipe) from time to time and mentally take stock of eating habits and make new resolutions!

Do not try to lose weight too quickly, but aim for a steady loss of about ½ lb. each week. In six months you will have lost a stone, with only a little cutting down of normal sugar and starch.

Slimmers' Sauce

This egg-thickened sauce can form the basis of many dishes, sweet or savoury.

> ½ pint milk
> 2 eggs, beaten
> 2–4 oz. grated cheese or 6–8 drops 'Saxin'

Scald the milk and pour over the beaten eggs. Return to pan and cook gently until thickened, stirring all the time. Season with cheese, salt and pepper, or with chopped parsley, etc. Or sweeten with sugar substitute and vanilla or other flavouring essence, and use as required.

Slimmers' Salad

This idea appeared in the *Sunday Express* and is re-printed by their kind permission. The ingredients below make enough for a complete day's meals for one person. The whole salad is made up in the morning and eaten as required during the day, thus saving much time and effort. Two such salad days during every week mean a weight loss of at least 10 lbs. in eight weeks, and it is a most delightful way of staying in good shape, as the salad really is one of the most delicious we have ever tasted. This can take the place of the two 'liquid days'.

Chop the following fruits coarsely and grate the vege-tables (raw of course) fairly finely, or chop them, and mix all together in a big bowl:

> 3 eating apples
> 1 large pear or 2 small ones
> 1 orange
> 1 medium-sized green pepper
> 4 carrots
> 4 sticks celery
> ¼ cucumber
> handful raisins

The salad may be dressed with a cupful of yoghourt and three teaspoonfuls of pure lemon juice if liked. This is a convenient way of slimming for those who take a packed lunch to work, because that portion can be simply put into a lunch box with a spoon all ready for eating.

Good luck with your slimming. We do hope that you have enjoyed the recipes in this book, and that the vegetarian way of life will prove to be as happy and healthy a one for you as it has been for us over three generations.

APPENDIX

THE WHITE EAGLE PUBLISHING TRUST

The White Eagle Publishing Trust is a charitable Trust created to publish the philosophy of the White Eagle Lodge and matters appertaining to it. The White Eagle Lodge works for the brotherhood and harmony of all life. It proclaims a way of life – a new religion, if you like – which is happy, harmonious and satisfying. Its philosophy supplies answers to many of the apparently insoluble problems of life today, and shows how every individual can help to alleviate suffering and improve conditions around him.

If you would like further details of this vital work, and a list of books published under the imprint of the Trust, please write to:

The White Eagle Publishing Trust,
New Lands, Liss, Hampshire, GU33 7HY.

OTHER USEFUL ADDRESSES

The Vegetarian and Vegan Food Guide may be obtained from:

The Vegetarian Society (UK) Ltd,
Parkdale, Dunham Road,
Altrincham, Cheshire.
or
53, Marloes Road,
Kensington,
London, W8 6LD

The aim of these societies is to promulgate a knowledge of the advantages of vegetarianism and full membership is open to all practising vegetarians who wish to support and help further this cause. Associate membership is open to those who, though not vegetarians, desire to help the work of the society. A copy of the monthly newspaper The Vegetarian is sent free to members and associates. Details of membership, book list and interesting literature may be obtained from the above addresses on request.

The vegetarian ideal of compassion towards life is at the heart of the Compassion in World Farming Trust, which is seeking to combat cruelty and ruthlessness in farming wherever it occurs. It offers sensible alternatives to those farming methods which are violent to the land (in the form of artificial fertilisers, insecticides, etc.) and cruel to farm animals and wild life. Members are kept in touch by regular newsletters. Full details from The Secretary, C.I.W.F., Copse House, Greatham, Liss, Hampshire, GU33 6HB.

Many women, especially vegetarians, feel repulsed at the thought of using beauty products made from substances which have involved pain and suffering to animals. It was to try and abolish such cruelty and to make known the attractive alternatives that the Lady Dowding founded Beauty Without Cruelty. Membership is open to all who would like to support her in this task. Write for details to:

The Lady Dowding,
1, Calverley Park,
Tunbridge Wells, Kent.

Beauty Without Cruelty now offers its own range of delightful cosmetics made from pure flower and vegetable products. These may be obtained from many Health Food Stores.

NOTE ON METRICATION

Most recipes in this book will convert easily to metric measurements. To do this, here are the approximate metric equivalents of the units used:

1 lb. is roughly equivalent to $\frac{1}{2}$ kilo;
$\frac{1}{2}$ lb. is roughly equivalent to $\frac{1}{4}$ kilo or 250 grammes.

For smaller measurements, I think it is easiest to take:

1 oz as being roughly equivalent to 25 grammes. For larger amounts, of up to $\frac{1}{2}$ lb., the 25 g. unit is easily multiplied, e.g. 2 oz. becomes 50 g., 6 oz. becomes 150 g. It must be emphasised that this is only approximate, but for the recipes in this book, except the cakes, it is usually accurate enough.

For liquid measurements:

1 pint is roughly equivalent to $\frac{1}{2}$ litre; the following other rough measurements can be used for smaller amounts:

$\frac{1}{2}$ pint is roughly equivalent to 250 millilitres;
$\frac{1}{4}$ pint is roughly equivalent to 125 millilitres.

The Celcius oven temperatures are also gradually being introduced. Here is a table of equivalents:

	°Fahrenheit	°Celcius	Gas Mark
Cool	200	93	$\frac{1}{4}$
	225	107	
Slow	250	121	$\frac{1}{2}$
	275	135	1
	300	149	2
Moderate	325	163	3
	350	177	4

Fairly hot	375	190	5
	400	204	6
Hot	425	218	7
	450	232	8
Very hot	475	246	9
	500	260	

We are indebted to Margaret Blatch, M.C.A., author of 'Household Non-Flesh Cookery', whose work has been our model and inspiration, and who has kindly given us permission to use some of her basic recipes; also to all our kind friends and family whose ideas, recipes and encouragement have resulted in this book.

INDEX